YOUR
LEADERSHIP
FOOTPRINT

First published in 2022.

ISBN: 978-1-86922-956-6
eISBN: 978-1-86922-957-3

Published by KR Publishing
Tel: (011) 706-6009
E-mail: orders@knowres.co.za
Website: www.kr.co.za

Typesetting, layout and design: Cia Joubert, cia@knowres.co.za
Cover design: Marlene De Lorme, marlene@knowres.co.za
Editor: Genevieve de Carcenac
Proofreading: Valda Strauss, valda@global.co.za
Project management: Cia Joubert, cia@knowres.co.za

YOUR LEADERSHIP FOOTPRINT

How will you be remembered?

Reflective questions on leadership
impact and executive effectiveness

Dave van der Merwe

kr
publishing

2022

DEDICATION

This book is dedicated to family and friends who have encouraged me to keep writing, especially my wife Esmé who has been a huge source of support during the writing of this book and my previous fiction novels.

TABLE OF CONTENTS

ABOUT THE AUTHOR

David J van der Merwe was born in the Karoo, South Africa and was raised in Nelspruit.

Dave is married to Esmé and they have two sons Calvin and Bradley. They reside between Pretoria and Plettenberg Bay.

Dave has broad and varied interests including writing, travel, bird watching, photography, camping, spending time in the Kruger National Park, cooking, fly-fishing, reading, walking, and playing golf. Dave and Esmé also lead a Life Group for their local church and they run a small annual charity event to support underprivileged orphans.

Dave experienced a life-changing event in his mid-twenties when he broke his neck playing rugby and narrowly escaped paralysis. This has encouraged him to live life passionately and to always have a positive outlook on life. This has also been instrumental in leading him to his life purpose of making a difference in the lives of others, and more specifically developing the leaders of the future.

Dave qualified as a Chartered Accountant and works in the management consulting industry. His passion however is leadership development and driving executive effectiveness.

Books by the author

Dave van der Merwe has also self-published three fiction novels under the pen-name of David Vander. These include:

Vander, D. (2018). *Shudder in the Wall: A story of deception and intrigue*. Johannesburg: Independently published.
Vander, D. (2019). *The Shudder Lingers: The intimidation and deception intensifies*. Johannesburg: Independently published.
Vander, D. (2020). *The Shudder Wars: Mastermind holds city to ransom*. Johannesburg: Independently published.

PROLOGUE

Leadership seems deceptively simple to explain, yet in its essence, it is multifaceted and complex. Therein lies its allure and the reason why thousands of books have been written on the subject, with each trying to find the silver bullet that demystifies it. I have always aspired to write my own leadership book, however, trying to distil the essence of leadership into a thought-provoking and yet practical book, has always been rather intimidating. Publishing three fiction novels certainly made the prospect of writing a leadership book less daunting.

This book deliberately seeks to be simple and light on theory. I have no doubt that many who read this book may have their own perspectives on each topic, and I am hoping that my experience and views will serve to grow the richness of your own leadership journey.

I have been privileged to work with many leaders throughout my career, some of them great, others good, and some rather dismal. One would think that the best lessons in leadership would only come from great leaders – yet over the years, I have come to realise that every leader has something to teach. When I sit back and reflect on numerous conversations with many great leaders around the world, I realise that I have gained invaluable insights into what great leaders do, what poor leaders teach, and how to leverage this for my own success. Whilst I use the term "*insights*" to describe leadership, much of it is often common sense, but the essence of leadership requires being human above all else.

The concept for this book emerged from an Executive & Management Coaching programme which I completed through the University of Cape Town, which highlighted the incredible value of asking powerful questions. Each chapter in this book is framed as a thought-provoking question, which allows you to self-reflect on your personal leadership style in parallel with my observations and experiences. What matters most, is what you do with the insights you derive from the self-reflection. Being deliberate and intentional about taking action could be the critical trigger required to drive a paradigm shift in your leadership journey. Each of the twelve parts of the book are also titled using a verb, again implying a call for action.

My sincere hope is that this book encourages you as you grow in your own leadership journey and the many critical moments that will ultimately define your path to success and, in due course, significance. I hope that this book will serve as a practical leadership companion, provide you with sage advice, and tangible solutions to leadership challenges, which will hopefully smooth your leadership journey. The views I share in this book are my own observations which, I hope, add to the allure and discourse on the intricacies of what leadership could be. I welcome any alternative views.

I also wish to emphasise that I have personally fallen short on many of the questions or insights over my career, but I hope my growing experience is accompanied by increasing wisdom and that my own leadership style is edging in the right direction each day, in the hope of emerging as a more effective leader. Some aspects of this book are grounded in my Christian beliefs, without which I may not have truly begun to actualise my own true potential and fulfil my greater purpose of developing others.

As Peter Drucker famously told Bob Buford,[1] "The fruit of your work grows on other people's trees." I hope that this book will contribute to a more fruitful harvest, and I wish you every success in the growth of your own personal leadership journey.

What is the leadership footprint you will leave behind?
How will you be remembered?

INTRODUCTION

This book is intended to serve more as a self-reflection guide than a textbook of good practice. Hence, this practical handbook for leaders is structured around a series of key themes and questions. The key themes are broadly reflected as follows:

- Self-Awareness as a Leader (parts 1-3)

- Leading Change and Talent (parts 4-6)

- Thinking Strategically and Stakeholders (parts 7-9)

- Enabling Execution and Driving Results (parts 10-12)

Each chapter starts off with a question designed for self-reflection, for which there is no right or wrong answer. After reading the supporting text, I would encourage you to return to the question, and reflect on whether your initial response remains unchanged. You might also wish to use it as a tool to ask colleagues or family members to provide their views of how they perceive your leadership. However, reflection and awareness are only the starting point. Taking action will guide you to become a more effective leader or executive.

Each question provides a key message in response to the question, a key action phrase, observations on the question and practical tools. The book also highlights some warning signals to look out for that indicate all might not be well. Obviously, should the opposite be true, then that will be a sign that things are going well. Some of the warning signals may repeat themselves in several chapters. Should any repeated warning signals resonate with you personally, it could be a prompt for deeper reflection, and corrective action.

I also flag that while the book often talks about business organisations, many of the questions, principles, ideas, and reflections are also applicable in other leadership contexts.

Below are a few key ideas that are considered in this book, although I encourage you to explore the detail so that you do not miss out on the richness of the dialogue.

- Living a balanced life

- Your plan for significance

- The importance of always being authentic and human

- How you show up as a leader

- Creating quality thinking time to shape the building blocks to an effective future

- Asking powerful questions

- Being deliberate and intentional, and taking appropriate action

- Focusing on what really matters and owning the narrative

- Unlocking the potential and discretionary energy of others

- Being an enabler for the whole ecosystem to flourish

- Working on the business, versus working in the business, and knowing when to be where.

Many of the questions and insights have come because of leadership experiences, which I have been privileged to facilitate for leaders all around the world. My observation is that experiential learning can be profound in terms of impact on leadership effectiveness. Whilst the book provides many invaluable ideas and concepts, I encourage you to make this learning experiential, by learning in the flow of work itself and applying these to your leadership journey.

Below is a summary of the key questions from each chapter:

- Part 1 - Reflecting on self
    - Are you living a balanced life?
    - Are you grounded by unshakable values?
    - Are you purpose-led, in life and work?
    - Do you lead a life of integrity?
    - Are you empathetic to others?
- Part 2 - Gaining perspective
    - Are you aware of how your leadership style is perceived?
    - Do you recognise the value of coaching and are you coachable?
    - Are you an influencer?

- o Are you deliberate in creating quality thinking time?
- o Do you know what limits you and what you should stop doing?

- Part 3 - Building leadership fitness

  - o Are you clear on what your top priorities are?
  - o Do you know where and what to focus on as a leader?
  - o Are you constantly curious, learning and seeking new ways of doing things?
  - o Are you resilient and able to lead through a crisis?
  - o Do you have access to a think tank or sounding board?

- Part 4 - Setting the tone

  - o Do you uphold the organisational values?
  - o Do you consistently live and demonstrate appropriate leadership behaviours?
  - o Do you allow for courageous conversations that challenge the status quo?
  - o Is your culture conducive to effective decision-making?
  - o Do you embrace frequent employee engagement?

- Part 5 - Driving team effectiveness

  - o Do you have a shared purpose that unlocks your teams' discretionary energy?
  - o Are you able to accurately articulate the team dynamics?
  - o Are you and those around you working at the right level?
  - o Are you deliberate in creating a collaborative working environment?
  - o Do you provide effective recognition for individual or team success?

- Part 6 - Unlocking talent potential

  - o Are you a catalyst in creating an environment that seeks to unlock people's full potential?
  - o Do you actively seek to find and grow people's passion and strengths?
  - o Do you openly encourage curiosity, innovation, and experiential learning in the workplace?
  - o Are you actively nurturing and developing your talent for future capabilities?

- o   Are you hiring the best possible talent when looking externally?

- Part 7 - Fostering relationships

  - o   Do you know who your key stakeholders are and what their needs are?
  - o   Is servant leadership a key principle in how you foster relationships?
  - o   Do you seek to build others up and make the community a better place?
  - o   Do you know your work colleagues at a personal level?
  - o   Do you really know what others want to achieve in life or career?

- Part 8 - Making strategic choices

  - o   Can all stakeholders in your organisation clearly articulate your purpose and aspirations?
  - o   Do you drive strategic choices that are aligned with chosen outcomes?
  - o   Can everyone consistently articulate your organisation's value proposition?
  - o   Are your resource allocation principles clearly defined and applied?
  - o   As leader, do you create context and own the strategic narrative?

- Part 9 - Creating shared value

  - o   Do most of your strategic choices lead to sustainable value creation for all stakeholders?
  - o   Can everyone in the organisation articulate the top five value drivers?
  - o   Can everyone in the organisation articulate the top five value inhibitors?
  - o   Are your incentives / KPIs aligned to sustainable value creation, or do they destroy value?
  - o   Can everyone in your business describe how the organisation creates value?

- Part 10 - Creating predictability

  - o   Do you frame powerful questions that improve predictability?
  - o   Do you have robust decision-making processes that lead to optimal decisions?

- o Is your business structured to ensure transparency of unfiltered information?
- o Does your performance management process deliver intended results?
- o Are you collaborating and focusing efforts to solve real business challenges?

- Part 11 – Driving effective execution
  - o Is there a tangible link between strategic intent and tactical execution?
  - o Do you consistently test end-to-end value chain execution effectiveness?
  - o Do you drive effectiveness through meaningful work?
  - o Do you focus on the right things and how well you are doing them?
  - o Do you run effective meetings?

- Part 12 – Managing risk and opportunity
  - o Can everyone in the organisation articulate the top five controllable risks?
  - o Are you confident that the risk mitigation is actionable?
  - o Are you prepared for a crisis and able to create opportunities from it?
  - o Do you have a mindset of managing controllable risk to zero?
  - o Do your lessons translate into improved execution?

PART 1

REFLECTING ON SELF

"Those who follow the crowd usually get lost in it."

Rick Warren

Answer the following questions as accurately as possible, trusting the intuitive nature of your first response. The bonus question is intended as an outside-in view.

Part 1 – Question summary	Totally disagree	Disagree	Neutral	Agree	Fully Agree
1.1 Are you living a balanced life?					
1.2 Are you grounded by unshakable values?					
1.3 Are you purpose-led, in life and work?					
1.4 Do you lead a life of integrity?					
1.5 Are you empathetic to others?					
Bonus question					
Would others agree that you lead with purposeful impact?					

Once you have read this chapter, revisit your responses above and assess whether your responses remain the same.

What does this reveal to you? What three actions or goals are you going to set yourself regarding these insights?

Question 1.1

ARE YOU LIVING A BALANCED LIFE?

⌗ *Key message*

Achieving life balance requires being deliberate in achieving an equilibrium across multiple spheres of life, for example spiritual, family, physical, work, mental and social. Note that I intentionally use the term *life balance,* rather than *work-life balance*, with the latter being a far more commonly used phrase. Life balance refers to gaining perspective of your whole being and making conscious choices about what, with whom, and when to prioritise each aspect of your life. You only have one life – live it well!

💬 *Key action phrase*

Make deliberate choices to create life balance.

⚠ *Warning signals*

- Working long hours
- Believing work and money are the key barometer of success
- Hearing those closest to you tell you to get your work-life balance right
- Feeling tired and not enjoying your job
- Searching for meaning
- Being called a workaholic

⚲ *Observations*

When engaging leaders on the topic of life balance, they will typically insist that they have work-life balance. Their initial responses of experiencing work-life balance, as opposed to life balance, always intrigue me. I often ask if their family would agree with their statement. Watching the back-peddling is fascinating! I believe leaders miss the point of life balance as opposed to work-life balance for two reasons. Firstly, they do not think that life could come first and secondly, they lack the awareness that their lives may be woefully out of balance. The reason why I believe that life should come first is that when everything is in balance, you are far more likely to have greater impact and be more significant to society. The harsh reality is that far too many of us quite simply do not have life balance, but rather work dominance.

Life balance is easier to understand when considered in the context of where individuals find themselves in the various stages of their life and career. These stages could include early ambition, career success, making an impact and then giving back. The early stages of ambition and success are often epitomised by hard work with long hours and sacrificing personal time and relationships. Therein lies the life-balance trap, as many individuals struggle to extricate themselves from the manic demands of work. This leads to work-life balance being out of kilter and ultimately impacting negatively on life balance. One often hears of retired leaders, businessmen, or family members who regret not having spent less time at work and more time living life.

How often have we heard a derivative of the following story? A middle-aged man is fishing, watching the birds and maybe enjoying a colourful sunset, when a young businessman dressed in a fancy suit asks the man what he's doing, to which he replies, "I've taken off the afternoon, and come fishing". The young man responds that he should reprioritise his life, work hard, and earn more money so that he can retire early, and then have plenty of time to go fishing. The middle-aged man just smiles, and replies, "Why not do both now?" This certainly is food for thought.

Eckhart Tolle in his book *The Power of Now*[2] summarises the concept of life balance well with the following question: "Are you waiting to start living? If you develop such a mind pattern, no matter what you achieve or get, the present will never be good enough; the future will always seem better. A perfect recipe for permanent dissatisfaction and nonfulfillment, don't you agree?"

To illustrate this, many leaders say that if they can just get through the next few weeks, then they will be OK. My response is that those are a few weeks of opportunity to live life differently. Be present now, rather than chase something too far in the future or spend time mulling over the past.

The issue of life balance, along with wellbeing and mental health, has certainly come under the spotlight during the Covid-19 pandemic. One thing the pandemic taught us is the value of reflecting often and assessing if you are living a balanced life, and if not, to prioritise life balance. It is vital for your health and sanity as a leader to live life now, so that your impact can in fact be amplified by being more present in the balanced aspects of your life. Refer to the *practical tools* section to identify where your shift in focus needs to be.

Finally, the following are a few considerations, other than those from the life balance diagram below, which can be a guide to improving life balance:

- Spend time with family and friends

- Take time out during your workday for a meal or a walk

- Take weekends off, and engage in sport or hobbies

- Utilise your annual leave fully – ideally you should have a leave problem, namely not enough of it

- Focus on positive things and positive people

- Identify what gives you joy and do more of that

- Laugh, and laugh some more

- Establish your maximum working hours per week (Forty hours is ideal, and fifty-five hours should be the maximum. According to the World Health Organisation, working fifty-five hours or more per week is a serious health hazard.)

- Periodically unplug from technology and media

- Find your "switch off" place, whether it is the bush, beach, or mountains. Renewal is essential if you wish to bring your best self to others

- Cut out time wasters (e.g., watching mindless social media or aimlessly scrolling through television channels) and negative people.

⚒ *Practical tools*

There are countless examples of a wheel of life, which seeks to visually reflect selected elements of a balanced life.

In this case I have reflected it as a table. For each element, use the scale of 1-5 to indicate where you currently find yourself, as well as where you aspire to be, to achieve life balance. A score of 1 is indicative of feeling dissatisfied and a score of 5 for satisfied. This will highlight where your life balance gaps are and will draw attention to where your deliberate choices for change could be.

Core element	State	#1	#2	#3	#4	#5	Choice or action
Character	Current						
	Desired						
Family & quality time	Current						
	Desired						
Spiritual balance	Current						
	Desired						
Physical/ health	Current						
	Desired						
Mind, growth & learning	Current						
	Desired						
Work & career growth	Current						
	Desired						
Financial wellbeing	Current						
	Desired						
Recreation & hobbies	Current						
	Desired						
Relationships & Social	Current						
	Desired						
Contribution & purpose	Current						
	Desired						

Question 1.2

ARE YOU GROUNDED BY UNSHAKABLE VALUES?

⊶ *Key message*

Every leader should aspire to lead authentically and consistently, while upholding unquestionable values. In today's increasingly public and socially visible world, being grounded by unshakable values is a non-negotiable trait for any leader. Any other superficial foundation will easily be visible and open to judgement, and your ability to be authentic will be readily exposed. Living according to upstanding principles and demonstrating infallible values is fundamental to becoming a great and trusted leader.

🗩 *Key action phrase*

Live and lead authentically and consistently, being grounded by unshakable values.

⚠ *Warning signals*

- Believing that you can authentically portray a value, which is not genuine

- Wearing a loud façade

- Demonstrating a disconnect between what you feel, say, and do

- Having questionable actions when under pressure

- Failing to have a belief system

⚲ *Observations*

Over time, I have observed two kinds of leaders: those who are grounded in rock-solid values and those whose values are loosely connected to dubious foundations. It may appear trivial to new leaders but being grounded makes a huge difference in how you live your leadership journey and the leadership footprint, or legacy, you leave behind. Whilst you may not always be aware of how you live your values, it is glaringly obvious to your followers, who seldom commit fully to a leader they cannot trust or one who demonstrates inconsistent values.

Leaders who are grounded in good values and authentically and consistently live by them, have a significant advantage over those who do not, in that they can lead others to more impactful and sustainable outcomes. Think about the leaders that you have worked for. If they were genuine and trustworthy, it is far more likely that you would have gone the extra mile to support them and committed your support to the business objectives that were agreed.

On the flip side, leaders whose values are loosely connected to dubious foundations tend to show their true colours when placed under pressure. As in all things in life, we have choices to make, and backing someone of dubious character is very seldom an option. Talented individuals rarely serve or follow leaders who do not espouse strong values and worthy principles.

Leading by upholding strong values is a deliberate choice and demonstrates strength of character. Stephen Covey, in *Principle-Centered Leadership*[3] states, "Effective people lead their lives and manage their relationships around principles." The absence of values or principles in your leadership journey is likely to result in disappointment and frustration.

Values tend to be an intuitive matter, often informed initially by how we were raised. As with any other leadership discipline, it requires deliberate effort to define what you stand for, and then deliver on your own self-imposed principles. I have observed that very few leaders have taken the time to define who they are and what they stand for. Being an effective leader requires you to deliberately articulate what your values are, being aware of what is non-negotiable for you, and then how you pitch up and emulate those values.

In this book I will often refer to "pitching up". This implies how you act or how you show up and how others will experience you. As a leader, you have a far greater likelihood of being trusted when you pitch up so that your actions and choices consistently align with your values, no matter how challenging the situation or circumstances. If your principles remain grounded and unshakable under fire, your character and impact will grow exponentially. It is also likely that as you grow as a leader, your values may evolve, with some becoming more important than others. Instead of comparing one value to another, it is the act of how you consistently espouse your collective value set that really matters.

For a leader to be authentic, you need to draw on your values, leading from your true self and having the courage to show your vulnerabilities. This builds trust. When others can relate to you as a person and know that you experience the same emotions they do, your ability to connect and build trust is that much easier.

It is also critical that leaders demonstrate the living of values, so that less experienced team members can see that it is OK to be consistent in their personal values, whether at home or work. This concept is also emphasised in Stan Slap's book *Bury My Heart at Conference Room B*[4] where he describes that if managers can't live their values at work, then they detach emotionally from their work. If this happens, it is a lot harder for them to bring discretionary effort to the workplace. Throughout this book I will refer to discretionary effort which implies that individuals will be emotionally connected to what they do, bring passion to the work, and use their full potential or capability.

Finally, my sense is that leaders who are spiritually grounded tend to leave a more significant impact on people and legacy. Don't let anyone else define who you are.

✖ Practical tools

The intention of this section is not to express which values are best, as each is unique to an individual, but rather provide reflective examples.

What is important, is the intent behind the words and how you live them in your life, and how you demonstrate those values in your capacity as a leader.

Below are a few selected examples of values. As you reflect on them, ask yourself:

- Can I articulate what grounds me and what I stand for?
- How do I compare against each example?
- Do my values remain consistent under pressure?

Examples of values and virtues could include:

- Honesty, empathy, respect, optimism, inclusion, friendly, polite, open-minded, caring, community, forgiveness, consistency, commitment, accepting, and resilience, integrity, reliability, gratitude, loyalty, trustworthy, courageous, self-control, compassion, fairness, cooperation, embracing and humility

Defining your values is easy. What ultimately matters, though, is how you act on them, demonstrate them in your life, and how others experience you. Leading is behaviour driven.

?

Question 1.3

ARE YOU PURPOSE-LED, IN LIFE AND WORK?

☞ *Key message*

Being purpose-led, knowing why you exist or why you do what you do, provides leaders with a powerful and liberating mindset. The sooner in life you find your true purpose, the more impactful you will be as a leader. Defining your broader life purpose is often linked to your life-stage, age, experiences, and where you find yourself in your career. We often hear of individuals who are facing a mid-life crisis, but my observation is that this is mostly about people seeking their greater purpose. It is also critical to be passionate about, and have an emotional connection with, your purpose. This should be the case in both life and work, thereby sustaining life balance. When you can live your purpose, and you feel passionate and personally fulfilled by it, that is what I would envision as a leadership sweet spot.

🗨 *Key action phrase*

Be intentionally purpose-led, in a way that positively impacts the lives of others.

⚠ *Warning signals*

- Driven by money, titles, and power
- The term "mid-life crisis" resonates with you
- Losing interest in work and lacking motivation
- Trying to find meaning in your life
- Struggling to get up for work, or anything for that matter
- Finding each day is another grind

♀ *Observations*

Finding your purpose in life is easier said than done. My general observation is that younger people struggle to find their purpose, not from a lack of trying, but rather that they need to experience more of life first, so that when they do seek and find their purpose, it is that much more impactful. There are, of course, many people who do find their true purpose earlier in life, so I hope my observation doesn't limit you in any way.

Finding your purpose takes time and effort, and is seldom something that comes easily, all wrapped in shiny paper with written instructions on how to implement it. Life simply doesn't work like that. In the practical tools below, I outline some thoughts that may help you find your purpose. My observation is that finding your life purpose is often easier for individuals who are spiritually grounded.

Being purpose-led as a leader gives you a significant advantage, in that you can make choices which are anchored to something bigger than any individual or idea. This may come as a surprise, but most of your followers will easily see right through any superficial façade you may create if you are not purpose-led. If you do not believe this, ask them. Those brave enough to give you feedback will not sugar-coat their opinions.

There are, no doubt, countless views, and books on the topic of purpose. In my opinion, purpose is fulfilling your God-given talent. It is therefore knowing why you exist and why you do what you do. This book focuses primarily on one clearly defined purpose or talent, namely leadership. This fundamentally means leading and serving, not yourself, but others. I repeat, leading and serving others. There can be no greater purpose than making a positive impact in the lives of others, unlocking growth, and watching each human being shine. Often the most fruitful years of your life are living out your purpose, making an impact, and living a life of significance by giving back. If your purpose is to lead, I encourage you to do so to with energy and to the best of your ability.

In addition to finding work that allows you to fulfil your purpose, it is important that your work is rewarding and that you are passionate about it. Being purpose-led and doing work that ignites a fire of passion in you, is an extraordinary place to be. Incidentally, most individuals will agree that they would want to follow a leader who is purpose-led and passionate, and they are also more likely to give them their discretionary energy and commitment. Undoubtedly, there will be some narcissists reading this who will disagree.

Imagine two brief examples: firstly, you are a leader who is passionate about making an impact in society, who leads a fulfilled life, and leads an organisation that fulfils its purpose, goals, and objectives in a sustainable manner. Secondly, you are a leader with no clear passion, you find life boring, and you lead an organisation that seeks to exploit the environment and doesn't give back to society. Which leader would you prefer being? Living life passionately, being purpose-led and making an impact, would be my choice!

If what you do doesn't excite you, then it is time to reflect and make different choices. It is tragic to observe how executives fall into a rut and are unable to extricate themselves from a career path, which ultimately leads to the mid-life crisis which I referred to earlier, and often years of unhappiness.

I take myself, as a Chartered Accountant, for example. For years I primarily focused on numbers, and I was often boxed into financial roles because of it. Deep down I yearned for something else. I decided to make a significant career change in my fifties. I studied further and made a quantum shift into leadership development. I was often reminded that I really should not do it. In our church life group, someone once said to me, "Don't let anyone else define who you are." Fast forward a few years – I am now living my purpose, and mostly doing what I am passionate about. Quite frankly, more accounting standards would never have ignited the fire within me.

One final thought: if you are truly struggling to find your greater purpose, Rick Warren[5] says, "To discover your purpose in life you must turn to God's Word, not the world's wisdom."

✖ *Practical tools*

I often encourage leaders to spend time writing down what they are passionate about and what their greater purpose is. It surprises me how often individuals have not done this simple exercise. Note that I used very particular words, "writing down". There is no real value in just conceptually thinking about it. There is extreme power in writing this down on paper. If it is not written down, then for all intents, it does not exist.

Establishing purpose is best achieved by spending quiet time, either in prayer or meditation, and seeking it out. What motivates you? Start by writing or journaling and do not be surprised if this takes days or weeks. It is not as simple as some would have you believe. Once you have landed on your purpose, it should resonate with you substantially, and you should be at peace with what you have articulated, and yes, it must be written down.

When considering passion, I often ask, what makes you excited to get up in the morning? What will get you out of bed to live life, or go to work?

The answers to both purpose and passion could be insightful to where you should refocus your life and where you should devote your energy. Once you have written down your purpose and passion, share it with your spouse or trusted friend. The act of communicating your purpose can often be quite revealing, rewarding and a spur to action.

I often encourage people to write down their ideal job description. What would you do, why would it be exciting, and could you do this for the rest of your life? I have seen many beautiful stories of how this simple exercise has changed people's lives for the better.

?

Question 1.4

DO YOU LEAD A LIFE OF INTEGRITY?

☞ *Key message*

Most people aspire to live a life of integrity and maintain the moral high ground. For me, integrity simply infers that there's congruency in your thoughts, your heart, your words, and your actions. All four of these need to be present for integrity to prevail, and for you to be regarded as trustworthy. By implication, in every situation, no matter how challenging, your integrity needs to be consistently experienced by others in your actions and reactions. Furthermore, it is essential that your integrity remains intact when no one else is present.

🗩 *Key action phrase*

Be trustworthy in everything you do. Maintain your integrity even under the most challenging circumstances.

⚠ *Warning signals*

- Believing that you have absolute integrity, but your reaction to situations is questionable

- Finding yourself saying, "I wish I had not said or done that"

- Knowing that you are not regarded as a trusted partner

- Twisting the truth to suit the circumstances

⚲ *Observations*

Your true intent is foundational to achieving integrity and aligns to a fundamental integrity choice for each of us, namely, is our intent whole-hearted, or not? This may seem like a superfluous question, but again,

I have observed, that many leaders say they value integrity, and yet when they need to pitch up, their true intent could be perceived to be questionable. Quite simply, if you do not have the utmost integrity in the moments that really matter, you may impair your ability to be an impactful leader.

I appreciate John Maxwell's[6] perspective on integrity: "Power really is a test of character. In the hands of a person of integrity, it is of tremendous benefit; in the hands of a tyrant, it causes terrible destruction." When I facilitate discussions with groups of leaders, I often ask, "How will you be remembered?" The response is always positive, but sadly the actions are not always as positive.

As mentioned earlier, for integrity to be real there must be congruency in your thoughts, your heart, your words, and your actions. Should you be facing a difficult situation, the litmus test will be in your final actions. We often hear the expression that children do not listen to what you say, but rather observe and do what you do. The same applies for any of your followers, peers, or subordinates. They will observe what you do with a microscopic lens, and any failure to be consistent, will influence them in making up their mind about who you are as a leader and whether they can trust you. Your followers may also start doing what you do, therefore the importance of being aware of your own integrity and the extent to which it is genuine, is essential.

Integrity and trust go hand in hand. It can take years to build integrity and trust, and yet they can be destroyed in an instant. If you find yourself in a challenging situation, take time out to reflect whether what you are about to do, or a decision you are about to make, will be done with utmost integrity. It is also useful to consider whether your response could be misconstrued, in which case, apply the twenty-four hour rule: think it over, sleep on it, and only then respond. You are then likely to make a better judgement call and hopefully uphold your integrity.

It is probably useful to demonstrate integrity with an example. Let's assume that you need to provide performance feedback where someone has fundamentally let the team down.

Lacking integrity:

- Thought – wow that was a lousy effort
- Heart – they should be disciplined
- Word – hey, it wasn't that bad, please don't do it next time
- Action – gossip at the coffee station about how pathetic the person is

Demonstrating integrity:

- Thought – wow they let the team down
- Heart – they should be coached
- Word – can we unpack what happened, so that you can improve next time
- Action – showing support by listening and guiding them to improve

Finally, it is always useful to reflect on your actions before you pull the trigger. How might it be perceived, experienced, and what are the unintended consequences. If things go badly, what will the news headlines say?

✘ *Practical tools*

The following questions can help build up a deliberate awareness of your integrity. In making key decisions or having to demonstrate action in any life or work situation, take a few minutes to plan the decision or response. Again, it is enlightening to capture your thoughts in writing.

- What are your thoughts on the matter?
- What does your heart tell you?
- What words should you consider using?
- How might you respond and what actions will you take?
- Will your response build the other person up or break them down?
- What is the risk of not taking action (doing something or nothing)?
- Are all your responses above in alignment?
- And finally, how will you be "judged" if it goes wrong?

This simple intent-alignment exercise can quickly point out if your initial decision or response is appropriate. If it gives you peace, then proceed. However, if there is a sense of unease or misalignment, this could be a trigger to rethink your decision or response.

It may also be useful to consider challenging situations that could arise in both your workplace and personal life. In preparing for such situations be deliberate in considering your response and formulating your actions so that your overall intent and integrity is kept intact.

Reflecting on these points could assist in building leadership muscle.

Question 1.5

ARE YOU EMPATHETIC TO OTHERS?

🔑 *Key message*

Actively demonstrating empathy to others is a powerful leadership trait which shows you care, increases human connection, and unlocks positive energy. My perspective on empathy is being aware of and connecting with others on a truly human level, while deliberately seeking to understand their emotional state. It also means being authentic and caring for others. As a leader, your awareness of how others are feeling, whether verbally expressed or not, is essential to becoming an impactful leader. Empathy as a leader also means letting go of your esteemed position, title, or ego, and realising that each person in your organisation is a human being, and maybe a parent, or sibling or child. True empathy cannot be faked.

💬 *Key action phrase*

Be authentic in engaging others to truly understand where their headspace is or how they feel. Caring enough to connect, human being to human being. *Be more human!*

⚠ *Warning signals*

- Allowing your individual ego or position to place you above checking in to see how others are doing or how they might be feeling

- Not caring about the other person; you just want the job done

- Not knowing anything about your closest colleagues

- Driving task over everything

- Unable to sense when someone is going through a difficult time

♀ *Observations*

Empathy is a lever which reflects who you are as a leader, and whether you truly care for others. Empathy can also be a key determinant of where you are on a spectrum from servant leader to an egocentric leader. Without going into a theoretical analysis of empathy, it simply means being aware of another person, taking the time to check in with that individual and truly listening to understand how that person feels.

Empathy must come from the heart. If you do not truly care for people, then quite frankly, showing empathy will be like pushing water uphill. Early in my career, my focus was mostly about the task and getting the job done. I really missed out on so much, like getting to know others and having a more human touch. It was only as I matured and started leading a life group for my local church, that I truly began to be aware of others, care for them, and show empathy. In my view, this lack of awareness of softer skills is a failing of education and society.

As I grow as a leader, I am becoming more aware of small signs that all is not well with someone. Sometimes it is reflected in their physical self, other times in their work. It never ceases to amaze me, if you are intentional about truly seeking to check on someone's emotional state, that you find out that they are suffering from something, have a family crisis, lost a loved one or have a family member who is critically ill. Taking that moment to truly connect shows empathy, but more fundamentally, says you care. In that person's eyes, you will be a leader they will readily follow.

Empathy takes effort. For some of us empathy may come naturally, but for others it is hard. "Walking in someone else's shoes" is an age-old proverb, but still holds profoundly true. Until you truly understand, you cannot judge. Demonstrating empathy requires effort from you as a leader. Be more aware, listen, observe, ask questions, and show compassion. Essentially, *be more human*, be more mindful of how you engage and treat others. Empathy is reliant upon levels of connection, situational context, and a safe psychological space to express care and concern.

It is interesting how the global pandemic that rocked the world in 2020, highlighted the value of empathy as a core leadership trait. Very few leaders had experienced such a universal challenge as that which was brought upon us through the coronavirus. In hindsight, leaders who showed genuine empathy outperformed those who did not. If we cast our minds back to that time and think of two Presidents, namely Jacinda Arden and Donald Trump, and how differently they pitched up on empathy. Arden showed empathy and rallied the country behind the pandemic.

John Maxwell, in his book *Everyone Communicates Few Connect*,[7] has a great quote: "People may hear your words, but they feel your attitude." As I shared earlier, true empathy cannot be faked. Most people can smell fake empathy from a hundred miles away. Therefore, making time to connect is essential. For many, this may seem like wasting time, but rest assured, showing empathy and connecting will pay handsome dividends, many times over.

In the same book,[8] Maxwell outlines five key practices for connecting with others:

- Connect by finding common ground
- Keep communication simple
- Create an experience everyone enjoys
- Inspire people
- Remain authentic throughout.

Finally, treat others as you would like them to treat you. Use empathy to engage and create emotional connection.

🛠 *Practical tools*

As a leader, some tips for nurturing empathy could include:

- Taking time to connect with individuals before starting a meeting, by having a quick check-in
- Being fully present and becoming more aware of others, what they say, the look on their faces, the emotions they display. The focus should be on them, not you

- Asking powerful questions that require a more considered response

  o   How are you experiencing this difficult situation? Or

  o   What are you grateful for?

      Not just:

  o   How are you doing?

  o   The response is typically "fine", followed by the unspoken thoughts of the boss: "thank goodness, now let's get to work".

- Ensuring that you remain focused on the individual. Avoid your phone and similar distractions

- Showing that you care, in your words and actions

- Becoming aware of what people are not saying

- Never showing fake empathy, as this will create harm when it surfaces, and is likely to destroy all the good you have done.

PART 2

GAINING PERSPECTIVE

"It is so easy to break down and destroy. The heroes are those who make peace and build."

Nelson Mandela

Answer the following questions as accurately as possible, trusting the intuitive nature of your first response. The bonus question is intended as an outside-in view.

Part 2 – Question summary	Totally disagree	Disagree	Neutral	Agree	Fully Agree
2.1 Are you aware of how your leadership style is perceived?					
2.2 Do you recognise the value of coaching and are you coachable?					
2.3 Are you an influencer?					
2.4 Are you deliberate in creating quality thinking time?					
2.5 Do you know what limits you and what you should stop doing?					
Bonus question					
2.6 Would those closest to you: family, work colleagues or social friends agree with your answers?					

Once you have read this chapter, revisit your responses above and assess whether your responses remain the same.

What does this reveal to you? What three actions or goals are you going to set yourself regarding these insights?

?

Question 2.1

ARE YOU AWARE OF HOW YOUR LEADERSHIP STYLE IS PERCEIVED?

⌐ *Key message*

Being aware of how your leadership style is perceived, or experienced, or the impact that it may have on teams, is often the subtle difference between good and great leaders. Given past success, many leaders may continue to assert their old leadership style, oblivious as to whether it is effective or not, and whether it remains relevant. Seldom do leaders take a moment to reflect on how effective their leadership style is in the current context, and what could be capitalised on. Even less frequently do senior leaders ask for feedback. Critical to awareness is the need to listen, and I stress, really listen. Only a handful will be open to soliciting feedback and making the changes necessary to become exceptional leaders.

🗩 *Key action phrase*

Be intentional about increasing awareness, asking for feedback about how your leadership style is being experienced, and be willing and intentional about making appropriate adjustments to your leadership style.

⚠ *Warning signals*

- Believing that given your leadership position, you do not need feedback

- Not caring about your leadership style, as you always get what you want

- Not caring about what others think

- Not making time for self-reflection

24

♀ *Observations*

Many leaders have ridden the wave of success, based on a particular leadership style which delivered the results they required. Such past success could create a blind spot, as leadership styles and expectations of leaders have changed significantly in recent years. This could be exacerbated for individuals who have power and may have led with an autocratic leadership style. This blind spot is commonly referred to as the hubris syndrome, which describes how power is associated with significant success in the past.

As with so many assumptions, things change, including how leaders are perceived, how their leadership style is experienced, and that which is expected of them as modern leaders. This could have a weighty implication for leadership styles in the current context. It is vital for you as a leader to pause and reflect on how your leadership style may be perceived.

Have you taken a few minutes to place yourself in the shoes of your teams or colleagues, and paused to think about how they may be experiencing your leadership style?

In conducting interviews for leadership development interventions which I facilitate, the diverse views of leadership styles as described by the leader and their direct reports or peers, are often so far apart, you would think they were talking about two different people.

A precursor to awareness about your leadership style is listening and observing. I believe that the most important aspect is to listen, with the intent of understanding that which is being said and being perceptive to the underlying messages. Listening is hard, and it takes consistent practice to master it. A good listener can identify both stated and implied messages and is able to observe if there is congruence between messaging and how it is portrayed by the speaker. Great listeners also reflect on what was not said. Effective listening can be a major differentiator for you as a leader. One technique in practicing intentional listening skills, is to replay that what you have heard being said, without judgement or any additional innuendos. As Stephen R. Covey[9] puts it, "Seek first to understand, then to be understood."

I would like you to reflect for a moment on two questions:

- If you were in a team of businesspeople, would you choose yourself as a leader?

- What might your colleagues think of you as a leader?

Given that such a reflection is probably riddled with personal bias, I believe that you need to be deliberate about asking for feedback. Before you do, however, you need to ensure that you are open to feedback and create a safe space with limited consequences, for meaningful feedback to take place. Without this psychological safety, you may only get what you want to hear, that is if you get anything at all. On the flip-side, creating an environment for honest feedback can be an extremely powerful catalyst for your personal growth, and importantly, for your effectiveness as a leader. Honest feedback can also potentially prepare you to handle future challenging leadership moments more effectively.

As Nancy Kline in *Time to Think*[10] says, "When you are listening to someone, much of the quality of what you are hearing is your effect on them." By implication, the quality of your listening to the individual from whom you are seeking feedback is critical and will translate into the quality of the feedback you get. It is also critical that you are respectful of the feedback. As Kline says, "Listening of this calibre ignites the human mind".

For feedback to be truly valuable, something needs to shift. It starts with your mindset and willingness to accept the feedback and make concrete changes or take steps towards implementing the changes required. This will create the building blocks for exponential growth in your leadership effectiveness. Failure to act on feedback will ultimately lead to unnecessary pitfalls in your leadership journey. In the various career roles, I have fulfilled, it was initially difficult to receive feedback, but honestly, I cannot imagine where I'd be without it. I'll use this moment to express my gratitude to the many wonderful colleagues that have given me honest feedback over the years. Thank you!

Knowing when to be right, humble or trust your intuition, is a critical awareness skill. We often hear the phrase "gut feel", which can be defined as an intuition or hunch that something isn't right or is not as it is made out to be. Gut feel is an indicator that something feels either good or bad, without having evidence of either. Whilst this is a powerful trait, it should not be the sole indicator of awareness. Some key complementary steps in trusting your intuition include listening to what people say, asking open-ended questions, reflecting on feedback, and creating time to think. Only then should you act.

Finally, throughout these steps indicated above, authenticity, candour, respect, and admitting mistakes on your part, are critical. In a nutshell, *be more human.*

✗ *Practical tools*

Asking for feedback requires intentional action on your behalf:

- Be prepared to listen to both stated and implied messages
- Make it safe for feedback to be provided. State clearly that there will be no negative consequences, as the intent is for your personal growth. This psychological safety is crucial to receiving honest feedback
- Be consistent in asking for feedback, not just when it is going well. For example, after every meeting, workshop, or key interaction, spend five minutes asking for feedback
- Ask open-ended questions:
  - What worked well? – amplify
  - Where can I improve? – start
  - What should I change? – stop
- Do not respond in the moment, as often a verbal response may be seen as being defensive, but rather ask probing questions if anything is unclear
- If possible, reflect on what is not being said
- Take action that demonstrates that you have heard and taken valuable feedback to heart. Actions speak louder than words.

Question 2.2

DO YOU RECOGNISE THE VALUE OF COACHING AND ARE YOU COACHABLE?

⌒ *Key message*

The value of a trusted advisor, mentor, coach or sounding board is essential to enhancing your leadership effectiveness, influence, and impact. Whatever connotations may have existed about executive coaching in the past, I believe that it is indeed a silver bullet to unlocking your full potential as a leader. It is inconceivable that any top sports star or team would compete without a coach at the highest levels. Why should it be any different for leaders of large organisations? Recognising the need for a coach is one thing, however, you also need to be coachable, be open-minded to feedback, listen, reflect, and take corrective action.

🗩 *Key action phrase*

Invest in your leadership impact by appointing an executive coach.

⚠ *Warning signals*

- Thinking that you can be effective without external input
- Believing that coaching is for under-performers only
- Not having a mentor
- You are successful, what could anyone possibly teach you?
- Thinking that you cannot teach an old dog new tricks
- Allowing your ego to deny you the benefit of a coach or mentor

⌕ *Observations*

During some of my most challenging moments as a younger leader, one of my mentors decided to invest in my career by appointing an executive coach on my behalf. At first, I was sceptical, after all I was forty, and going places, or at least so I thought. In hindsight I now realise that my progression as a true leader would have stagnated, due to a gap in my softer human skills. Having a coach was one of the best things that ever happened to me. I have subsequently benefited from other coaches who have made an indelible impact on my life, both personally and on my character. In particular, Elana Godley opened my world to new possibilities as a leader, and she always reminded me, "*Be Dave*". Thank you for this, Elana.

What do Larry Page, Sergey Brin, Mark Zuckerberg, Sheryl Sandberg, Tim Cook, and Jeff Bezos have in common, besides all being successful leaders of iconic business which we all know well, and can't live without? In Trillion Dollar Coach[11] it is revealed that they all consulted Bill Campbell, who was without doubt the most influential executive coach in Silicon Valley in his time. If coaching was pivotal to the success of these iconic leaders, then that should be a powerful signal to each of us. When I reflect on the leaders I work with, by far the majority are already successful, indicating that they recognise the value of external insight for growth.

As mentioned earlier, it is inconceivable that any sports star or team would achieve their full potential without investing in a coach. Note, the intentional use of the word investment, not expense. Investing in yourself for growth will create lifelong returns. Over my career, I have been privileged to work with many board members, c-suite executives, and senior management. Initially I found it surprising when esteemed leaders told me how lonely it is at the top of an organisation. I now know this to be a harsh reality. A business leader is often expected to know all the answers and cannot appear weak. This places undue pressure on them and should be a light bulb moment to get a coach or, at a minimum, an external mentor who is there to support their leadership effectiveness journey.

Prior to elaborating on the benefits of coaching, you need to answer an all-important question: Are you coachable? This is no trivial question, and I have observed that some leaders have such a huge ego, that they are uncoachable. Leaders may also be uncoachable if they have very low self-awareness and are blind to the need to grow and develop further. They believe they have all the answers and do not need someone else to hold up the mirror to who they truly are. Those with such an attitude would likely not read this book. These leaders will often be described with words that are not complimentary. How will you be remembered?

Coaching has a myriad of advantages. The list below reflects a few.

- It creates a safe space for the leader to explore and share thinking
- It allows the coach to ask tough and thought-provoking questions
- It allows someone to hold up the mirror to the leader
- It allows for honest feedback and encouragement
- It creates awareness, that can be tested and reflected upon
- It allows for your hopes and fears to be freely expressed, without judgement
- It allows for the leader to test assumptions and what needs to be changed
- It allows for the planning of appropriate actions
- Importantly, it creates a trusted advisor and often a life-long friend

If any of this resonates with you, appoint an executive coach, and witness the impactful outcomes that can be achieved. I so fundamentally believe in the power of executive coaching and leadership development, that I changed careers in my mid-fifties to assist existing and future leaders in unlocking their potential and driving their effectiveness.

⚒ *Practical tools*

Executive coaches often have a preferred coaching framework, and there are a variety of effective coaching frameworks out there. One of the simpler and easier approaches is the GROW model, which was created by Sir John Whitmore. This can be used both by a coach with a leader, or by the leader with their reportee. The GROW model in the context of a coaching session has four key steps:

- Goal – what is the performance goal, objective, problem to solve, or decision to take?

- Reality – what is the context, reality, assumptions, or perspectives?

- Options – what are the options, choices, solutions, or new possibilities?

- Way forward – what are the action steps, obstacles to remove, or things to experiment?

In the absence of a coach, there are some helpful reflection tools for self-development. One that I value is the Gibbs Reflective Cycle, based on the framework first created by Professor Graham Gibbs.[12] This model allows you to learn from situations that you may be experiencing. This model has five easy steps:

- Description – what happened?

- Feelings – what were you thinking or feeling?

- Evaluation – what was good or bad about the experience?

- Conclusion – what else could you have done?

- Action – if it happened again, what would you do differently and what would you amplify?

?

Question 2.3

ARE YOU AN INFLUENCER?

☞ *Key message*

It is always interesting to observe how certain individuals in large organisations and teams, are positive influencers with broad impact, regardless of their formal titles. This subtlety is important for aspiring leaders. To make a sustainable impact as a leader, you need to be a positive influencer. Attributes that drive influence could include being authentic, asking questions, listening, being interesting, showing empathy, being curious, and generating ideas. Influence is earned over time and no position guarantees a leader's real or perceived influence. Earning influence requires a certain maturity, often aligned to a greater purpose, that demonstrates that you are there for the greater good of people, the organisation, and broader stakeholders.

🗩 *Key action phrase*

Be intentional about becoming a leader who serves for the greater good and seeks to provide wisdom that benefits all.

⚠ *Warning signals*

- You believe that your position of power entitles you to an opinion or to be included as an advisor

- You are seldom contacted / asked for a point of view

- People often ignore what you say

- You are outspoken on many topics, but often ignored

♀ *Observations*

Many leaders aspire to that enviable position of being a trusted advisor, influencer, and go-to person for a point of view, question, or solution. It is interesting to observe that each organisation has a formal structure and an informal, more influential network. A tell-tale sign is that before a key decision is made or a policy is changed, someone would say, have you asked Mr Joe or what would Mr Joe think of this? Being such a network influencer is a powerful leadership trait and a powerful lever to create impact.

Influence is about the strength of individual relationships and your credibility with other people in the organisation, who themselves have credibility. Your influence is amplified through the network of those who trust your opinion and views. Influence is not something you force, but rather getting others to behave and act in a positive way.

Some of the defining traits of an influencer that you as a leader can develop or amplify:

- Be an authentic leader who is trusted, which speaks to your character

- In all your interactions, you need to demonstrate integrity

- Your answers must demonstrate that you have considered the impact for the collective good

- You use powerful questions to unhook others (see later in the book)

- You demonstrate that you have applied your mind

- You actively listen to other influencers

- You encourage systemic thinking, which demonstrates impact and understanding of unintentional consequences

- You learn from the past, and apply to the current

- Your point of view conveys true wisdom

- You are fair and ethical

- You see the big picture and can show others new possibilities

- You explore new possibilities and are open-minded

- You know when to use other influencers to positively drive change

- You know what others need

This list is not exhaustive, but points to wisdom and intent. Some of these traits take years to cultivate, so treat your influencer position with the care and respect it deserves.

There is always a risk of naming influencers, as things can change rapidly. However, a few will illustrate the point. In my view, positive influencers include Nelson Mandela and Warren Buffet. Negative influencers are often a lot more prevalent, just think about business leaders who led huge corporate collapses or disrespected politicians all around the world. I return to a key question: How will you be remembered?

I would also like to highlight the issue of influence versus positional power. It is often surprising how an executive has great ideas but is reluctant to execute them because they perceive that their position does not permit them to act. It is almost as if they believe they can only make a difference if their position or title permits it. I see this as a self-imposed value-trap. I always say, *don't let anyone else define who you are* and do not let them limit your potential. Great influencers do not rely on permission, title, or the biased opinion of others.

I would also like to point out that I'm not advocating game playing or using a position of power to unfairly influence or sway something. This is inherently about having a positive impact beyond yourself. As a leader, your influence should be about abundance and everyone benefitting. As Stephen R. Covey[13] says, "Win/Win is a frame of mind and heart that constantly seeks mutual benefit in all human interactions." Being an influencer brings responsibility, accountability, and ownership, therefore use it wisely.

If you have a natural talent to influence and make a difference, please do not waste it. The world would be a poorer place if nobody influenced anything or anyone. Therefore, if you have true and positive intent, exert your influence as widely as humanly possible. It is then that magic happens.

⚒ *Practical tools*

Suggesting practical tools to become an influencer is difficult, so I have tried to simplify it. A few steps include:

- Be clear on your intent as an influencer – it must be for mutual benefit

- Define for yourself how you would aspire to be an influencer and write this down

- Test how you currently show up against your definition of an influencer

- Test yourself against the selected traits shown earlier, to which you can add, and assess how you pitch up

- Bring your human side

- Reflect on the gaps and where you can take corrective action

- Finally, take action to grow your strengths or close the gaps which potentially hold you back the most.

The next best thing to you being an influencer, is to identify and spend time with the network of influencers in your team and organisation. Ensuring that you are connected, engaged, and aligned to such influencers is yet another powerful leadership tool.

Interested readers may want to read books by Dale Carnegie or Carol S. Dweck.

?

Question 2.4

ARE YOU DELIBERATE IN CREATING QUALITY THINKING TIME?

⚷ *Key message*

Quality thinking is undoubtedly one of the greatest value-enhancing functions of a leader, and yet surprisingly, it receives a disproportionally poor focus. Creating quality thinking time to work on the business is one of the most important things that should be prioritised in your diary. Quality thinking should be primarily focused on strategic thinking and the leader-led changes required in your organisation. This implies getting out of the details and switching off to the noise of meetings, emails, and endless conference calls. Creating quality thinking time is an action that requires you to do something very specific.

💬 *Key action phrase*

Be deliberate in creating quality thinking time in your normal working day. A minimum of four to six hours per week is recommended.

⚠ *Warning signals*

- Your diary is controlled by others

- You do not have blocked time for strategic thinking

- Your day is filled with emails, noise, and non-essential activities

- You seldom find time to think

- You reflect on the week, and realise that it was a mindless blur of wasteful activity

☿ *Observations*

What do I mean by quality thinking time? Firstly, it is quiet time that is set aside for you to think strategically about your business and the key drivers that will take the business forward and secondly, how you will drive the leader-led change to make it work. It also fundamentally means that you need to be in control of your diary, to create meaningful chunks of time to fulfil one of your most crucial roles as a leader. Some suggestions are offered below under practical tools.

I often ask leaders if they are deliberate in creating quality thinking time to think about their roles or the organisation itself. The most common response is, "I am too busy". My response to this is, "If you are not doing the strategic thinking for your organisation or business unit, who is?" The look on leaders' faces and their responses are often revealing, concerning, and at times even amusing. Creating quality thinking time requires a deliberate choice by you as a leader. It is not something you can ignore and definitely not something you can delegate.

To make a meaningful impact requires at least four to six hours per week, with a minimum of two hours at a time. One executive told me that I was mad when I suggested four hours a week, as he was just way too busy. My response, "Are you then doing the job you are mandated to do?", was not well received. Despite the initial protest, he did try it, and I recall a text a few weeks later stating: "This quality thinking time thing really works." Some leaders even set aside as much as eight hours a week. As a point of clarification, it does not just have to be you on your own. There can be circumstances where you choose to brainstorm a business challenge with a selected team of fellow leaders or managers. The key is that it must be quality thinking time, fully removed from the nuts and bolts of running the organisation.

As mentioned earlier, there are two key elements for quality thinking time to be effective, firstly the problem you are solving for, and secondly, how you as leader will create or facilitate the change. A few examples of the problem you are solving for could include strategy, strategic initiatives, transformation, execution effectiveness, a major business challenge, or even a new business direction. A few examples of the leader-led change could include explaining the "why" of the change, articulating the narrative that supports the change, defining leader-led ways of working, engaging colleagues, or actively participating in the change management process.

Counter-intuitive as it may seem, investing in quality thinking time makes the rest of your work exponentially more effective. I must emphasise that quality thinking time should be part of your normal working week and part of your job. Remember, your intention should be life balance!

Nancy Kline says in *Time to Think*,[14] "In fact, to take time to think is to gain time to live." In her book Kline also goes on to indicate that the quality of anything we do, depends on the quality of thinking we first do. This is profoundly important, because in the absence of quality thinking, both your strategy and supporting change narrative, could be directed, and swayed by someone else. It is your job to think, influence, and shape the outcomes you desire.

If you take anything out of this book, let it be a commitment to quality thinking time. Many leaders who I have worked with will recall me writing on a board – QTT – quality thinking time. This could be your single biggest lever for effectiveness. Through my leadership work QTT has become a critical leadership action and a widely used acronym in among my clients.

⚒ *Practical tools*

These practical suggestions are intuitive, and seem simple, and yet are seldom implemented. A few suggestions:

- Establish which time of the day you do your best thinking (morning, midday, or afternoon)

- Establish whether you prefer to do quality thinking in shorter bursts (two hours) or longer sessions (three to four hours)

- Deliberately block that time in your diary and be extremely protective of it (reminder to advise your personal assistant)

- Switch off business as usual interrupters (mobile phone, emails etc)

- Choose a place which leads to your best thinking (garden, comfortable chair, office with a whiteboard or coffee shop)

- Decide what strategic issue you will focus on, and then focus (strategic initiative, key decision, policy, through leadership etc)

- Ensure that the weekly habit becomes embedded as your way of working

- Enjoy the fruits of your thinking efforts.

?

Question 2.5

DO YOU KNOW WHAT LIMITS YOU AND WHAT YOU SHOULD STOP DOING?

⌐ *Key message*

A key lever to improve leadership effectiveness is awareness of what your blind spots are. Many leaders are often unaware of what limits them or holds them back. This can be a function of either lack of awareness or more likely being too busy to pause and reflect on this essential issue. Personal reflection and creating feedback mechanisms are critical to understanding where you are not effective or where your effort is being marginalised. Once that is clear, the next critical step is to create a stop-doing list, and then to be deliberate about stopping those things. Stopping non value-adding activities, can be a key enabler for creating time for quality thinking, referred to earlier.

💬 *Key action phrase*

Create awareness of what limits you and be intentional about creating a stop-doing list.

⚠ *Warning signals*

- You are frustrated by your diary

- You feel that many meetings are wasteful

- You do not get traction on a key piece of work

- You feel like your progress is hampered

- Your career often stalls

♀ *Observations*

This section focuses on blind spots regarding your time and energy, whereas leadership blind spots and biases are covered in other sections of the book.

In my interactions with countless leaders, the creation of a stop-doing list is initially met with scepticism, until they pause to reflect how some activities limit them in reaching the full potential their roles require or even their personal objectives. Sometimes letting go is hard to do. One of the key observations that allows the reality to sink in, is a simple question, "Does your diary reflect the work expected of you in your role?" Sadly, the answer is mostly, no.

Being aware of what limits you, what your blind spots are, and what you should focus on is a vital lever to improve your leadership effectiveness. Whilst asking you to be aware of what limits you sounds easy, we sadly develop habits which are hard to recognise unless flagged by someone else. If you are not clear, ask your colleagues, direct reports, or peers. They often know and will happily tell you if it is safe to do so. It is vital that you are aware of, and can articulate, what limits you.

In addition to external flagging, another key action is reflection and becoming aware of what you spend your time on and how you spend your time. We all know that time is precious, so why do we so liberally waste it on endless meetings, mindless social media, emails, or inefficient distractions? A key consideration is stepping back and being clear about what is required of your role and what the business outcomes are that are required. Be deliberate in clarifying what really matters.

Next is to be clear about where you should be focusing your attention. Do you need to be in every meeting you are invited to? Can the meeting be shorter? Is the activity you are doing linked to what you should be doing? These types of questions should all point to what your role is, the key expectations and the desired outcomes. Once you have this view, it makes it easier to focus on what really matters.

Many leaders would readily agree that they need to be more focused, until they are told that they need to stop doing certain things they have done to date. "I'm happy to create focus, but..." Let me be clear, unless you let go of the things that limit you, you cannot grow, move forward, or fulfil your true role. Creating a stop-doing list, and then being deliberate about stopping those things, is of paramount importance. My observation is that one easy way to start, is to cut down on non-essential meetings. Once you have a view of your stop doing list, it becomes easier to delegate those tasks or activities to others. Stop wasting your valuable time resource.

Quite frankly, the time saved because of your stop doing list will be exponential in the outcomes you can achieve through focus, and who knows, you may even find more time for quality thinking or generating life balance.

Perhaps another way to view this is to think of all the distractions we should not be doing. Either we ignore them, or we unwittingly accept them, which leads to a downward spiral of self-destruction and wasted effort. This point is emphasised by the following quote from William James: "A great many people think they are thinking when they are merely rearranging their prejudices."

Therefore, be deliberate and consistent in using your time optimally.

Practical tools

Some considerations to reflect on:

- What do you spend your time on and how do you spend your time? Analyse your diary
- Reflect on where you should create greater focus
- What drains your energy and adds no real value?
- Ask for feedback on where others perceive you waste time
- Create a stop-doing list of things or activities you should simply terminate
- Learn to say "No."
- As a final reflection point – does everything you do really matter?

PART 3

BUILDING LEADERSHIP FITNESS

"A leader is one who knows the way, goes the way, and shows the way."

John Maxwell

Answer the following questions as accurately as possible, trusting the intuitive nature of your first response. The bonus question is intended as an outside-in view.

Part 3 – Question summary	Totally disagree	Disagree	Neutral	Agree	Fully Agree
3.1 Are clear on what your top priorities are?					
3.2 Do you know where and what to focus on as a leader?					
3.3 Are you constantly curious, learning and seeking new ways of doing things?					
3.4 Are you resilient and able to lead through a crisis?					
3.5 Do you have access to a think tank or sounding board?					
Bonus question					
3.6 Would your colleagues agree that you are building leadership fitness?					

Once you have read this chapter, revisit your responses above and assess whether your responses remain the same.

What does this reveal to you? What three actions or goals are you going to set yourself regarding these insights?

Question 3.1

ARE YOU CLEAR ON WHAT YOUR TOP PRIORITIES ARE?

⌐ *Key message*

It is well-known that by creating a laser sharp focus on four to five key priorities, and executing well against those, then the likelihood of success and effectiveness increases exponentially. The concept of focus or priorities has been around forever, and yet many leaders struggle with prioritisation and where they channel energy in their personal, and work lives. This means doing the most important big things first. By implication, this also requires an appropriate allocation of time and effective delegation to others.

🗩 *Key action phrase*

Be deliberate in allocating most of your time to your most important priorities.

⚠ *Warning signals*

- You are distracted by many urgent things
- Your emails get your attention first
- You are drawn into countless meetings, that you really should not be in
- You never get the big things done timeously
- Your to do list grows daily
- You feel overwhelmed and procrastinate
- You miss important deadlines

⚲ *Observations*

The concept of priorities is well articulated in the various versions of the story about the professor, glass jar, rocks, pebbles, and sand. I won't repeat the whole story here, (google if required), but the crux of this story is that filling a glass jar with sand first, think urgent wasteful activity, will not allow you to get the rocks into the jar, i.e., the most important priorities. However, if you fill the jar with the rocks, think most important priorities, then the pebbles, then the sand, everything will fit into the jar. In other words, by focusing on the big important priorities first, it will allow you to attend to everything else, and manage your finite time resource, for ultimate effectiveness. I always like the idea that once you have a full jar, pour coffee in, and it will create more space. So, regardless of all the busyness, you can still make time for coffee, or a beer, connecting and building valuable relationships.

In an earlier chapter I dealt with quality thinking time, which can be used to think about the most important problems to solve, solutions to find, business outcomes to achieve or obstacles to remove. In addition, the importance of input from business, colleagues or an external facilitator is critical, as there is a natural tendency to be biased in our own personal view of what a priority is or should be, and many individuals will drift to priorities that fall within their comfort zone. Therefore, thinking about the problems, solutions, outcomes, or obstacles, requires challenging questions, reflection, and wrestling with their importance, to ensure that meaningful priorities are established. Ideally, the number of priorities should be no more than four to five, otherwise it again creates the risk that your energy or focus is being diluted.

In my work with leaders, a few key principles stand out.

- Priorities should enable the business to drive strategic priorities and lead change
- At least one priority should be focused on driving the leader's own personal effectiveness
- At least one priority should be about people and growing talent
- Priorities should be narrowly focused, as there is often a tendency to lump things together, which again limits your effectiveness.

Often, leaders will grapple with the prioritisation process, being afraid that they might omit a key aspect of their perceived role. My experience with this is simple, that if the chosen priorities are directionally correct in terms of the business strategy or individual growth, then it is good enough. What is far more important, is that the leader creates deliberate focus, and if done well over a six-to twelve-month time frame, then the improved effectiveness will make the selected priorities successful and deliver results. Then, once a priority has been delivered, you can integrate a new priority. Quite frankly, you are more likely to be effective doing five things well, than doing twenty things with mediocrity or a hundred things poorly.

Warren Buffet is famous for his 5/25 rule which requires you to list your top twenty-five goals or priorities. You are then required to select your five most important priorities. The remaining twenty items are placed on a secondary list. Buffet then implies that your top five goals should receive your full attention, and the remaining twenty on the secondary list should become an "avoid at all costs" list. Whilst not always possible in most organisations, you cannot argue with Buffet's success.

Once you have a view of what these priorities are, two other key aspects come into play, firstly, know when to delegate and secondly, identify the "*stop doing*" items, mentioned in an earlier chapter. This will be essential if you want to ensure appropriate emphasis on your identified priorities. Learning to say no might also become a key requirement, and, some may even proclaim, a game changer.

I have also observed that leaders struggle with the idea of zooming in on a maximum of five priorities, especially in today's manic business environment which is often swamped with seemingly endless demands, all portrayed as important and urgent. Besides the obvious culling of wasteful meetings, a useful approach is to rethink how you optimise your attendance in meetings or any other interactions. This is achieved by using each opportunity to drive the priorities you have chosen. So rather than sitting in a meeting, being steered by whatever the topic is, reframe your approach to see how you can use the topic or meeting to help drive your priorities. I am not suggesting that you bully the meeting to your agenda, but rather being savvy and using the meeting to shape thinking, create leader-led change or execution plans for what is important, as far as your priorities are concerned.

For example, if you have chosen a priority "capability development", and you are attending an executive committee meeting with the topic of operational efficiency, then there is a likelihood that the conversation could be very operational or tactical, around processes or systems. You could engage in the conversation by framing a powerful question such as, "If we were to be transformational in operational efficiency, what future capabilities should we be developing to create step-change?" Question 10.1 later in the book deals with the concept of powerful questions and has further examples. The reality is that if every executive is clear on their priorities and focus, everyone will win and the organisation will be better off.

Finally, to enhance the prospect of success, it will require you to dedicate about fifty percent of your normal working time to your priorities. In my experience, every leader who has consistently applied this approach will vouch for the exponential effectiveness they have experienced in their leadership journey. This fifty percent excludes quality thinking time.

✖ Practical tools

A good place to start is to consider the most important problems to solve, solutions to find, business outcomes to achieve, or obstacles to remove. From this it is likely that you could easily list twenty to thirty key priorities, which will include many of the activities currently on your radar and to do list. With support from a colleague or facilitator, take those and either discard marginal priorities or select those with the greatest impact. The use of a simple urgent/important quadrant can be used to narrow down the priorities. The objective is to end up with a maximum of five priorities in the very important/very urgent quadrant. These five priorities should be what really matters in the context of your role in the short-term.

Once you have those five priorities, allocate the time, define the outcome, determine how you will measure success and identify the key milestones required to execute on each priority. Being clear on the outcome increases the probability of success.

?

Question 3.2

DO YOU KNOW WHERE AND WHAT TO FOCUS ON AS A LEADER?

⚷ *Key message*

The concept of working on the business versus working in the business, has been around for a while and is used by many leadership experts. The essence of the concept is two opposite lenses; either you are focused on thinking holistically about the business, its direction and strategy, or you are caught up in the nuts and bolts of the day-to-day business. Whilst it is important to distinguish between the two, it is just as important to know when to work on the business, and when to drop into the detail, and work in the business. My response to leaders who are too deep in the detail is, if you are not doing the strategic thinking about the organisation, or working on the business, then who is?

💬 *Key action phrase*

Be clear about working on the business versus working in the business and knowing when to be where.

⚠ *Warning signals*

- You are caught up in the details of the business

- You are caught by surprise on big issues, and it feels like crisis after crisis

- You do not have time to think about the business strategy

- You are frustrated by the constant chaos of your job

- You are reactive when critical issues occur

- You are fighting fires all the time

💡 *Observations*

Do you know where, when and what to focus on as a leader? At first glance, this may appear to be a trivial question. Before reading further, are you clear on the answer?

I have often posed similar questions in leadership interventions, and a clear, crisp response never seems to easily roll off the tongue. The lack of certainty in responses from leaders is no surprise and is often defended with excuses such as inadequate time, a chaotic schedule, too many meetings, firefighting, and not meeting business performance targets. My view is that this is often a case of lack of clarity of when to work *on* the business versus working *in* the business. In my experience, as leaders move up the ranks, they hold onto what they were good at, which is often working in the business. Therefore, working on the business can be a challenge. This is often also seen with start-ups or family owned businesses.

A colleague and I recently facilitated a group of twenty country CEOs, and the most dominant phrase was "fire-fighting." When I challenged them that they were not being effective, I was met with a strong challenge. As the day progressed, and the concept of working *on* the business versus working *in* the business started to land, I could see the realisation dawn for many of those in the room. Finally, one CEO raised a hand, and stated, "I'm banning the use of the word fire-fighting in my business." Many nodded in agreement.

A critical leadership capability is knowing when to elevate the thinking and when to deep dive into the business, and the best results are achieved when these two diametrically opposite approaches are balanced and tailored to the context of the business at any point in time. What is equally important is the ability to comfortably transition from one mindset to the other. Let me unpack this a bit more.

Working *on* the business implies taking a much more systemic and holistic view of how the business functions, while also applying an outward-in approach and forward-looking focus. An outward-in approach implies thinking about the business from the customer's perspective and asking: "What value are we creating for our customers to remain competitive in the market?" I associate "working *on* the business" with the strategic thinking that is required to drive growth and outcomes. Selected examples of working *on* the business activities could include:

- Purpose and culture

- Strategic direction and objectives

- Sustainable performance

- Growth and capital allocation

- Value proposition and business model

- Leadership capability and growing human talent

- Capabilities and operating model

- Business transformation, which could include digital adoption

- Innovation.

Working *in* the business implies taking a more detailed view of the nuts and bolts of the business, often internally focused and in the present month or financial year. I associate "working *in* the business" with the operational and tactical activities that keep the existing business functioning optimally. There are, indeed, times when a leader must delve into the detail, to support a problem, crisis or to provide insights. Selected examples of working *in* the business activities could include:

- Operational or tactical activities

- Driving people related activities

- Employee value proposition

- Processes and systems

- Operational and functional excellence

- Cost reduction or asset efficiency

- Continuous improvement

- Reporting and governance

- Monitoring and tracking.

Any successful business requires both the strategic thinking and operational execution to function optimally. As a leader, you need to be very deliberate in your choice of working *on* the business versus working *in* the business, and importantly when to be where. Earlier, I referred to the transition between the two. Enhancing your effectiveness as a leader requires you to not only do the strategic thinking but being able to create the bridge back to operational execution, which requires you as a leader to articulate the strategic narrative, drive leader-led change and create context for others to make the connection between what they do on a day-to-day basis, and how that links back to achieving long-term sustainability. Select examples of the bridge between working *on* the business and working *in* the business activities include:

- Articulating the strategic intent

- Storytelling

- Driving leader-led change

- Engaging employees and stakeholders to drive change

- Creating clarity for the building blocks required to move from the present to the future

- Driving innovation, diversity, inclusion, and collaboration

- Establishing new ways of working.

An important observation is that working *on* the business often creates thinking that either improves how business works or removes critical obstacles. Therefore, working *on* the business often leads to improvements for those working *in* the business – a subtle point and yet profound point many busy leaders often miss.

In summary, the role of the leader is to think strategically, lead change and drive execution with people, but more importantly, to be aware of where your focus is at any point in time and to know when to be where. Again, I emphasise if you do not do this for your team or organisation, who will?

🛠 *Practical tools*

Take time to consider your organisation's context, the strategic thinking required, how to lead change and when to drive execution, using the earlier examples as a starting point. Be clear about what is required from your role and allocate appropriate time to each. This also creates a powerful link to the priorities described in the previous question. Again, a key driver of success here is allocating time for each job to be done.

A useful reflective exercise is to analyse how much time you spend on the examples mentioned earlier:

- Working *on* the business

- Working *in* the business

- Working the *bridge* between.

A further suggestion for effectiveness is not to mix these activities. For example, do not use the same meeting to discuss strategy and operational execution. While this may work for efficiency (managing diaries), it doesn't work for effectiveness (driving outcomes).

?

Question 3.3

ARE YOU CONSTANTLY CURIOUS, LEARNING AND SEEKING NEW WAYS OF DOING THINGS?

⊶ *Key message*

Being curious must be one of the most enduring leadership qualities you can have in your effectiveness arsenal. I have no doubt that if you are not genuinely curious, then you will become irrelevant, sooner rather than later. If we look at today's rapidly evolving world and business environments, you will realise that lifelong learning is imperative, not an optional extra. Along with curiosity, being open-minded to new ideas and ways of doing things, is increasingly important. As a leader, learning, being curious, and a having a growth mindset is essential, given the vital role you play in creating context for others.

🗩 *Key action phrase*

Be constantly curious, open-minded, and accepting that there will always be better ways of doing things.

⚠ *Warning signals*

- You are closed to new ideas or doing things differently

- You do not ask questions

- Your team or organisation hold the view that you know best

- You cannot understand why you should change what is working well

- You believe that nobody knows your industry better than your management team

- You do not think you can learn new things

♀ *Observations*

I went to university a long time ago, and to be honest, if that was the only knowledge I had, I would long since have been irrelevant. While university taught me some core thinking skills and work ethic, all it did was lay a foundation for future learning. While a tertiary education is viewed as essential today, it paves the way for a lifetime of learning, if, and only if, you want it. It is a choice. I often come across two types of individuals, those who rely heavily on past education and those who are constantly curious. There are no prizes for telling which person might be frustrated in their career, and which one is fulfilled and growing.

For those leaders who have been around long enough, before smart phones, we had basic mobile phones, and before that, only landlines. The reality is none of us want to go back to using landlines and fax machines. Learning is forced onto us in many ways. It is a simpler choice to want to be curious and learn, rather than be forced to change, sometimes when it is too late. Therefore, being curious, open-minded, and having a continuous learning orientation, reflects a growth mindset that is essential for a fulfilling a meaningful career. Being curious means being aware that we have limitations on how much we know, regardless of our experience or tenure in the business world. As Carol S. Dweck says, "A growth mindset is belief you can develop abilities." As stated often in this book, it is a choice, and it requires action from you.

My father always used to say, "When you get to thirty and look back at when you were twenty, you realise how little you knew when you were younger". This continues when you get to forty, and look back at when you were thirty, and quite frankly this cycle never stops. It is only as you grow wiser, that you appreciate how sobering this advice is.

Being curious, learning and building experience requires time and constant effort. Importantly, it also requires a mindset shift, asking open-ended questions, seeing things from different lenses or perspectives, and practising intentional listening. This is not rocket science – either you want to grow, or you do not. I have also observed that as we get older, it becomes more challenging to learn. Consequently, we defer learning until eventually it is too late. The best advice is to make it a daily or weekly activity, setting time aside to focus on learning, reading, or asking questions. As a leader, you create and set the tone for a learning organisation, so be aware of how you as a leader could potentially stifle growth. And by the way, learning new things might make you more interesting.

Closely linked to curiosity and learning, is being open-minded to new ideas and ways of working. You cannot expect a different result if you keep on doing the same things in the same way. As individuals, we often have limitations in thinking, however the value of collective knowledge, team innovation and connecting the dots, is where the real value lies. This means harnessing the full potential of ideas, concepts, approaches, and ways of doing things, from others, both internally and externally. It is well documented that the power of a team in solving problems, driving solutions and innovating, far outweighs what any individual can achieve. Of course, there are always individuals who will prove to be the exceptions to this.

Therefore, your role as a curious and learning leader is critical, but even more important is creating an environment for curiosity to thrive within your organisation. The tone for a learning culture starts at the top. Equally important is being open to external ideas, thinking or challenge. I have observed how leaders are fixated with a narrow industry view, when great ideas can be found in other industries and adapted into your organisational context. Again, be open-minded to new ideas from anywhere. One only has to look at many business disruptors, to see that ideas can come from anywhere and successfully transform entire industries. Examples include Amazon, Uber, and Airbnb.

Finally, it is essential to create the time for curiosity and learning. As Stephen Covey[15] says, "We must never be too busy to take time to sharpen the saw." My experience is that unless you are deliberate about life-long learning, you will become exponentially less relevant and useful.

✖ *Practical tools*

Some simple practical tools could include

- Curiosity – asking others for their perspectives and using open-ended questions (see examples under question 10.1)

- Learning – setting aside time to learn incrementally, but consistently, at least daily, or weekly

- Read widely and engage brilliant minds and thinkers

- Self – listen without judgement, read new things, and seek new perspectives on key topics

- Internal – design collaboration activities that solve real business issues

- Teams – create teams that are diverse in thinking and experience

- External ideas – bring in guest speakers or external facilitators to bring fresh thinking.

Question 3.4

ARE YOU RESILIENT AND ABLE TO LEAD THROUGH A CRISIS?

⌐ *Key message*

The global pandemic of 2020 threw the entire planet into crisis, with resilience on both a personal and leadership level, cast into an unrelenting spotlight. Resilience describes the ability to bounce back from a challenge, and emerge, either as you were before or strengthened to tackle the next challenge. Resilience also implies that as an individual or leader, you can see beyond the immediate crisis and articulate the building blocks that make you stronger, better, adaptable, or move you forward. It speaks of enduring, articulating hope and providing clarity on the steps required to get to the future. A resilient leader must empathise with the team during the crisis, acknowledge the critical issues, but also provide unwavering clarity on what must be done to move beyond the crisis, coupled with consistent support and understanding.

🗩 *Key action phrase*

Be deliberate in the strategic thinking and the building blocks required to move beyond the crisis, and then articulating the narrative on how to move forward.

⚠ *Warning signals*

- The organisation is paralysed in a crisis

- There is lack of clarity on next steps

- The words which prevail are crisis and firefighting

- The organisation experiences high levels of uncertainty which breeds fear

- There is a lack of empathy
- The crisis sets the organisation back badly, and recovery takes years

♀ *Observations*

The ability for a leader to recognise that the organisation is in crisis, is vitally important. The global pandemic of the early 2020s was a crisis which was obvious to us all. We all observed global leaders in the early days of the pandemic. Some denied the virus, whilst others immediately recognised it and took appropriate action. The impact of these two opposite approaches was visible for the world to see, and the results were alarmingly diverse. Sadly, it is no different in organisations. Key obstacles to resilience are leaders who are in denial, and this can be exacerbated by an overly positive ego. Therefore, the awareness of where an organisation finds itself is of the essence.

Equally important is the awareness of leaders in making sense of the circumstances and creating context for others. It often surprises me to observe teams who are in crisis and how they feed off each other's negativity, and how difficult it is to step above the immediate issues and contextualise what is happening. Leading in a crisis can be challenging, as there are harsh realities to be dealt with, often fuelled by negative energy. Leaders need to balance the acknowledgment of the reality with the need for realistic optimism and hope.

For a leader, this means making sense of immediate events while also considering the future. This links closely to a previous chapter of working *on* the business versus working *in* the business. The need for a leader to create context and articulate this clearly, is profound, as both immediate actions and long-term decisions will have a significant impact on the organisation for years to come.

Whilst the immediate attention is on the actual crisis, it is imperative that this does not paralyse the organisation. Great leaders focus their attention on moving the organisation beyond the immediate crisis and articulating the building blocks that allow them to improve the organisation and even flourish after the crisis. Again, quality thinking time is a key tool for leaders. Therefore, clarity on which actions are required immediately to stem the crisis, medium term actions to stabilise the organisation and then longer term building blocks or options that will ensure sustainability.

A leader's ability to help the organisation make sense of the crisis and contextualise actions for the organisation, are invaluable to sustainable success. Resilient leadership requires significant emotional intelligence, other than the tangible actions described earlier. The enduring qualities which stand out include empathy, reality testing, impulse control, stress tolerance and optimism.

The ability to show empathy and bring a *human* touch during a crisis is super-critical. My sense is that fabricated empathy will fail and will not galvanize an organisation to move beyond the crisis. To quote Daniel Goleman, "True compassion means not only feeling another's pain but also being moved to help relieve it." Lack of empathy will most likely lead to a downward morale spiral, and ultimately destroy value for all stakeholders, including clients, employees, communities, shareholders, and all other relevant partners in the eco-system. Empathy and reaching out on a human level, is vital. Being able to connect with people will ensure that you win their hearts and minds, thereby ensuring that the heavy lift required to move beyond the crisis is supported. That is where exceptional leaders succeed in a crisis.

Emotional awareness of the leader's own thoughts and biases is equally important, as are the biases of fellow leaders, teams, and the organisation. This is fundamental, as it is likely that critical long-term decisions, often in the absence of adequate information will be made during the heated moments of a crisis. We often hear the expression, "Never make a long-term decision in a short-term crisis", but the reality is that key decisions must be made. Hence the ability to be emotionally aware of biases is important.

Closely linked to this is to robustly challenge assumptions, so that decisions are better informed. This infers testing assumptions and assessing whether they hold true amid the crisis and whether they will stand the test of time. I flag this, as often assumptions are made in a crisis, and become entrenched which can negatively impact the organisation under normal circumstances.

I have observed that leaders who set direction during a crisis, listen to understand, show empathy, understand the biases, and take no regret decisions or options, are more likely to increase the probability of success. These decisions or options should not lead to regret, regardless of changing circumstances. So, in hindsight, you would make the same call. Importantly, this cycle needs to be repeated often as a crisis unfolds.

Building on the theme of leadership fitness, in an article by Timothy Tobin[16] he indicates, "Achieving peak leadership fitness requires self-awareness, goal setting, following a game plan and overcoming challenges." The article compares leadership to a marathon, which supports the topic of resilience.

⚒ *Practical tools*

Building on the above, some traits of resilient leaders that take the organisation beyond the crisis could include:

- Demonstrate empathy first and foremost

- Maintain composure despite challenges

- Lead with emotional intelligence

- A mindset that they will overcome the crisis

- Make decisions with less than perfect information

- Positive mindset that allows them to bounce back

- Focus on the immediate crisis and the building blocks, and know when to be where

- Retain energy, physically and mentally

- Seek new opportunities to benefit from the crisis

- Manage their emotions

- Be human

- Bring optimism and reality

- Maintain hope, often from a strong spiritual base.

Leaders could harness this in several ways.

- Reflect on their own leadership resilience against these traits
- Reflect on their approach using a past crisis for example
- Anticipate a future crisis and devise a response plan using the traits.

Leaders need to remind themselves that they should think of the benefits of being positive versus the downsides of being negative during the crisis.

Question 3.5

DO YOU HAVE ACCESS TO A THINK TANK OR SOUNDING BOARD?

☞ *Key message*

I strongly believe that we become more effective leaders when we engage others as trusted advisors and have a sounding board, who we can access to stress test ideas, theories, or key decisions. For clarity, by sounding board, I mean a group of people, rather than a board of directors. Being a leader is often very lonely. In my engagement with C-suite leaders, I am often surprised by how many leaders voice their loneliness or isolation, as all stakeholders expect them to have all the answers, when in truth they may not. When probed, it is often a self-inflicted limitation or being afraid of being perceived to be weak or ineffective.

🗩 *Key action phrase*

Be deliberate in finding trusted advisors who support you in decision-making or act as a sounding board for critical strategic thinking.

⚠ *Warning signals*

- You believe that it is a weakness to have a sounding board

- You believe that only your views count

- Your ego does not allow you to ask for advice

- You are not comfortable being vulnerable or admitting you don't know something

- You believe that you have all the answers

- You do not have someone that you can test ideas with

♀ *Observations*

In my engagement with leaders, I have repeatedly been told that the worst part of a C-suite leader's job is the loneliness. This often leads to the privileged opportunity to provide a safe space for leaders to share their thoughts, frustrations, fears, and hopes. The leader benefits by having someone listen to their ideas and stress test their thinking, and of course I benefit from the incredible insights I gather from countless leadership conversations.

In question 2.2 I dealt with the coaching which focuses on unlocking potential, whereas in this section I deal with a trusted advisor, which could be defined by some of the characteristics below:

- Mutual respect
- Candour and transparent conversations
- Vulnerability and willingness to show weakness
- Ability for both to listen intently
- Provide affirmation and encouragement
- Have requisite skills to engage on the relevant topic
- Willingness to call bad behaviour or narrow thinking
- Smarter than yourself

I believe that leaders can increase their effectiveness by being deliberate in creating trusted advisors for the various key roles they need to fulfil, whether it is strategic thinking, leading change, enabling execution or driving results. The first decision a leader must make in this regard, is the willingness to accept that trusted advisors can make a crucial difference, both to the leader themselves and ultimately for the benefit of the broader organisation. By not having trusted advisors, leaders deprive themselves of the opportunity to build richness into their leadership style and impact.

Next, a leader needs to be clear about what trusted advisors are required for. This could include strategic choices, change management, key decisions, talent issues, fresh thinking, business transformation considerations or it could be about the leaders' own personal leadership behaviours, effectiveness, and capabilities. Therefore, being clear about what is being solved for and what the outcomes are, will guide what type of trusted advisor should be engaged. Where possible, seek out advisors or mentors who are experienced, bring different views, able to hold up the mirror, are more mature or smarter than you.

Based on the business or personal need, an appropriate advisor or group can be established. These could include subject matter experts, colleagues, cross-functional teams, mentor, external executive coach or even a think tank group. A critical consideration, is that whoever is engaged should be an advisor that the leader can trust, is comfortable with and that the chemistry between the leader and the advisor works. While the latter point is important, depending on the role of the advisor, sometimes the leader needs someone with a different lens, so that appropriate challenge can result in the best possible outcomes.

Leaders need to be open to challenge, ask questions and listen, for the trusted advisor relationship to add value. Receiving advice is only part of the solution. A leader needs to discern the thinking, contextualise, and take action, to truly benefit. Ultimately, the leader must make and own the final decision.

Outside of the business environment, I have observed how successful leaders are part of a small think-tank for sharing ideas, asking questions, and debating issues. It is often an unrelated trigger from such a group that can solve complex issues or spark wildly successful innovations.

⚒ Practical tools

Establishing a think-tank or sounding board can take a variety of forms, depending on what the purpose is, as described in the observation section above. Examples could include:

- Informal think-tank gatherings

- Focus groups related to a specific topic

- Like-minded friends that meet to explore thinking or ideas

- Formal appointment of advisors

- Cross-functional teams formed for a specific purpose
- Breakfast meetings with mentors.

Framing questions for such sessions are a critical success factor. The problem being solved, and the question being asked to solve for the problem often dictates the success of any such thinking process.

Questions can be asked in different ways, and can be open, reflective, hypothetical, reflective or closed. Therefore, how the framing question is asked, will determine its effectiveness and the response that the leader may receive. Below are examples of a similar question, using different question types.

- Open: What options should I consider in this decision?
- Probing: For this decision, I have considered *the following*. What else should I consider?
- Reflective: If I made this decision, what might happen?
- Hypothetical: If I made this decision, how might others react?
- Closed: I have made a decision on the most promising outcome, does everyone agree?

As you can see, these questions are similar, but how they are asked impacts how trusted advisors could respond. The more open the question and relevance to the answers you are seeking, the better.

There is also merit in open-ended creative discussions which simply explore possibilities.

PART 4
SETTING THE TONE

"The price of greatness is responsibility."

Winston Churchill

Answer the following questions as accurately as possible, trusting the intuitive nature of your first response. The bonus question is intended as an outside-in view.

Part 4 – Question summary	Totally disagree	Disagree	Neutral	Agree	Fully Agree
4.1 Do you uphold the organisational values?					
4.2 Do you consistently live and demonstrate appropriate leadership behaviours?					
4.3 Do you allow for courageous conversations that challenge the status quo?					
4.4 Is your culture conducive to effective decision-making?					
4.5 Do you embrace frequent employee engagement?					
Bonus question					
4.6 Would the organisation change the culture you believed in, if you left?					

Once you have read this chapter, revisit your responses above and assess whether your responses remain the same.

What does this reveal to you? What three actions or goals are you going to set yourself regarding these insights?

Question 4.1

DO YOU UPHOLD THE ORGANISATIONAL VALUES?

⚷ *Key message*

In my experience, culture has been massively understated regarding its impact on building great organisations. Shared organisational values are what shape the culture. You will likely agree that people are attracted to a great organisational culture, but equally, good people will leave an organisation with a poor culture. It is important for leaders to appreciate that the culture should be about the institutional values that are accepted and lived by the people, and not the ideas or behaviours of ever-changing leaders. Leaders should place great importance on the values of the organisation, and if found to be inadequate, redesign it with collective involvement.

💬 *Key action phrase*

Be intentional about collectively designing and nurturing the organisational culture that broadly connects hearts and minds.

⚠ *Warning signals*

- There is a disconnect between what your organisation's values are and how people show up

- The organisation has unexplained staff churn

- People describe the organisational culture as toxic

- Your organisation struggles to retain top talent or cannot attract good talent

♀ *Observations*

Given that culture is intangible, many leaders, investors and board members have in the past disregarded the importance thereof, and its role in driving sustainable value. The corporate world is strewn with examples of both great and poor cultures, and how culture has ultimately defined the long-term outcome and success of organisations. Given that values shape culture, it is critical that the values must align to the organisational purpose and enable the strategy. If not, then they are probably not the correct values. Designing culture cannot be left to chance.

Values provide the compass and principles that leaders and the organisation need to uphold. They provide the guiding principles which define the organisational culture, which in turn is the fabric which binds the organisation together. When values are worthy and tangible, then they can be the catalysts for deliberate action and purposeful execution. There is ample evidence to suggest that values drive superior performance and results. Values need to be simple, intuitive, and easily relatable for all individuals, regardless of organisational hierarchy.

Beware the leader who tries to change the values. I say this because, quite frankly, I have seen far too many egotistical leaders who think they are the culture, and what they say goes. There is ample empirical evidence of how such leaders have destroyed entire organisations and sadly, the lives of innocent people. Dear Leader, you are a custodian of the organisation's values and culture. Lead and handle it with care. How will you be remembered?

I am also not saying that where values do not drive the right outcomes, they should be left untouched. A leader should assess values and how they motivate or demotivate people. Then working together with the whole organisation, lead the changes required that result in mutually beneficial outcomes for everyone. Your role as a leader is to uphold the moral compass and lead the organisation to greater heights. This is a key leadership responsibility, and rest assured, history will judge whether you upheld it, or not.

I re-emphasise that the values belong to the organisation and the best values are those which are cocreated and owned by everyone. Only when every individual believes that the values represent the collective, will they be responsible with the values, be accountable for them and own them. This will be a solid foundation for a great culture. If you agree with this view, then the role of the leader is simply to uphold them, live them and encourage them to new heights.

Finally, it is one thing to live the values, but that is not the same as how they might be experienced by others. Great leaders will self-reflect, seek feedback, and take corrective action, as appropriate.

🛠 *Practical tools*

In thinking about designing or improving organisational culture, it should address a few key elements, namely:

- Align to the strategy and strategic objectives
- Align to the organisational purpose
- Describe the aspirational culture outcome
- Articulate the appropriate behaviours
- Describe relevant ways of working
- Identify value moments

Call out bad behaviours (like the warning signals in each chapter)

A generic example could be:

- Strategic objective – exceptional client experience
- Purpose – empowered employees that make a difference
- Culture outcome – human centric in all we do
- Behaviour – empathy
- Ways of working – two-way employee engagement
- Value moments – when doing performance reviews
- Bad behaviours – talking behind each other's backs.

Question 4.2

DO YOU CONSISTENTLY LIVE AND DEMONSTRATE APPROPRIATE LEADERSHIP BEHAVIOURS?

⚿ *Key message*

In my experience one of the most important functions of a leader, is consistently living and demonstrating appropriate leadership behaviours. Your behaviours, how you show up, and your leadership style set the tone for a harmonious rhythm in an organisation. Your behaviours are the life-blood for a healthy cohesive environment and are the pulse that shapes the culture. Your leadership behaviours, conscious or unconscious, drive the culture. The more authentic and real your personal leadership behaviours, the more successful you will be as a leader.

🗩 *Key action phrase*

Think, speak and act according to the leadership behaviours your organisation demands, and those you expect of others.

⚠ *Warning signals*

- Your leadership behaviours are good, until the pressure is on, then your true colours rise to the surface

- You believe the culture in your team isn't great

- You are known as a bully

- You believe that those below you do not portray the best behaviours

- You can feel the office politics

⚲ *Observations*

I have mentioned this before, but there is an old an adage that says a child is more likely to do what you do, than do what you say. As a leader, you are being closely watched, whether you like it or not. Every moment of the day, people are listening to what you say, but more importantly, they are watching how you act, what you do and how you treat people. Consequently, how you show up, is a key factor which ultimately determines your success as an inspiring leader of people. When I reflect on my own personal journey, I fully accept that some of my leadership behaviours in my early career, were not good, and in hindsight, I could have taken earlier action. Thankfully, it is never too late.

While values shape culture, it is leadership behaviours that shift culture. Your leadership behaviours define who you are as a leader and how you will be remembered. Unless you are aware of your values and your personal brand of leadership style, your behaviours can be a blind spot. I have worked with multiple leaders who are often unaware of a particular behaviour, which sadly holds them back, thereby limiting their effectiveness. Driving your own personal leadership effectiveness requires you to set the bar high on values and behaviours. Aim low, and you get what you get. Therefore, it is essential that this aspect of your leadership receives deliberate attention and focus. It is the leadership footprint you leave behind, and how others will tell your story.

Before you can hope to be a great leader in the organisational context, you must show up at a personal level. This paragraph repeats some earlier text, which only serves to emphasise its importance. Having established your personal values and behaviours, strive to live it, authentically and consistently. Living your behaviours requires action, which includes, thinking it, meaning it, speaking it, and doing it. Any disconnect between the mind, heart, word, and actions, will show up as phony. If in doubt, be open-minded, ask for feedback and act on it. And, importantly, if you do seek feedback, take it on the chin and respect the person for giving you vital input for your success. Being open to that feedback is paramount in enhancing your leadership style and creating a more cohesive culture. People often leave an organisation because their leader or manager demonstrated a poor culture. So, it is in your interest to be deliberate about how you show up.

Defining appropriate leadership behaviours in an organisational context, requires intentional effort from the top down. I often engage with executives who say they have a culture issue, and that the behaviours from subordinates are problematic and need to be urgently addressed. Quite frankly, it is often not a culture issue, but a leadership issue, or to be blunt, a lack of leadership and misguided behaviours. As Harold S. Green says, "Leadership is practiced not so much in words, as in attitude and in actions."

Leaders must design the appropriate collective behaviours which they seek to expect in the organisation. Importantly, the designed behaviours need to be stress-tested for unintended consequences, using both an inside out, and an outside in approach. Once behaviours are designed, then they must be intentionally lived, day in, day out, especially in challenging circumstances or when you are under pressure. These behaviours need to be practised and become consistent habits at a leadership level.

It is also essential to create an environment where anyone can challenge a leader's behaviour and call out poor behaviour. If you are serious about creating a vibrant culture, then feedback is a vital building block. Making it safe for feedback to be provided may be a challenge, but the enduring benefits are well worth it.

When leaders are clearly demonstrating the desired behaviours on a consistent basis, only then do you consider cascading it into lower levels of the organisation. Cascading behaviours require thoughtful consideration and are not something that can be delegated to a functional role or junior staffer somewhere in the organisation. In other words, walk the talk, and not talk the walk.

Finally, remember, leadership behaviours are a game changer, and start, and end with you.

🛠 *Practical tools*

Define your personal values and leadership behaviours, align to the expected organisational leadership behaviours and be deliberate about it. Living leadership behaviours is all about habit. In defining your leadership behaviours, consider the following:

- What is the outcome I'm seeking? E.g., collaboration

- What is the associated behaviour? E.g., asking open-ended questions

- How will it be experienced? E.g., different views will be considered

- In which moment will it have the biggest impact? E.g., in cross-functional team meetings which break down organisational silos.

A simple practical tool is to have the desired leadership behaviours printed and laminated on a small card. At the end of each day, take a minute to reflect on the leadership behaviours and how you lived them and ask yourself the question – how did I pitch up today? Did I walk the talk?

I am restressing an earlier point, that there is great value in asking for feedback on the understanding that psychological safety is in place. This creates growth for all parties concerned.

Question 4.3

DO YOU ALLOW FOR COURAGEOUS CONVERSATIONS THAT CHALLENGE THE STATUS QUO?

⛏ *Key message*

Countless corporate disasters have occurred, simply because the organisational culture did not allow for courageous conversations or for constructive challenge and allowed a culture of fear to reign. As a leader the more you encourage courageous discussions, constructive challenge, and robust debate, the more your organisation will be resilient and grow, often exponentially. Clearly, you need to establish principles or protective guidelines, but courageous conversations are bitterly needed in all organisations. The benefits are diversity of thinking, improved solutions, better decisions, more effective execution and dramatically improved customer and employee experiences.

🗪 *Key action phrase*

Create an environment where robust conversations, constructive challenge, and diversity of thinking are actively encouraged, accepted, and embraced.

⚠ *Warning signals*

- The organisational culture does not allow for challenge
- The loudest voice wins
- The most senior person calls the shots, without challenge
- A culture of fear exists and is pervasive, throttling reality
- Strong disagreement is only expressed in the corridors

☝ *Observations*

Not allowing courageous conversations or constructive challenge to take place can often result in a culture of fear, with two unintended consequences, either poor decisions, or information which is often sugar-coated as good news. Unfortunately, desperately needed honesty and reality is replaced by a good news culture. The result is often messy, with millions lost in stakeholder value.

As a leader, you need to foster an environment where it is OK to have courageous discussions, where constructive challenge is accepted and where robust debate is encouraged. Whilst it may feel counter-intuitive, it establishes a fertile culture from which positive business outcomes can grow. In the absence of such an environment, a leader becomes less and less open to change. We have all seen the consequences of organisations where a larger-than-life leader has led an organisation to a tragic demise.

It is interesting to observe leaders who do not think such an open environment is worth it. I sometimes get the response, "Quite frankly, I think by now I should know what's good for this business." My response might be, "Is it possible that you may have missed vital information or is it possible than someone in your business has an idea that can revolutionise the organisation? Is it possible?" This is often met by a stony silence.

To create a conducive environment and reduce the negative impacts of a culture of fear, it is critical that leaders create psychological safety, which creates an environment where it is OK to speak up, without fear of negative consequences. In the Culture Code,[17] Daniel Coyle talks about embracing the messenger, so that when bad news or a different view is raised, then, "In these moments, it is important not simply to tolerate the difficult news, but to embrace it." Only leaders can create this safety.

Whilst such an environment lays the foundation for possibilities, it is essential to agree the principles or protective guidelines for such an environment, to ensure that it is done with good intention and not used to manipulate. If applied to critical moments, the intangible value created, is priceless. Examples of such principles could include:

- Being open-minded

- Being respectful

- Not being judgemental

- Showing empathy

- Putting yourself in the other persons shoes

- Asking open-ended questions

- Active listening

- Accepting that there might be another way

- Upholding respect for others

- Tabling the facts.

Courageous conversations can be fostered by establishing ways of working that allow for this to take place. These conversations should encourage all parties to be asking questions, expressing their views, receiving feedback, and then reaching a mutually acceptable conclusion.

Constructive challenge can be harnessed in group or team sessions to unlock the best possible outcomes. The challenge must be guided by the principles mentioned before. The danger here for leaders is not the challenge itself, but rather your own awareness and emotional maturity. If you see each challenge as a personal affront, then you are doomed. If, however, you see this as a genuine challenge to seek the best solution or best decision, then you will reap the benefits.

Diversity of thinking can be harnessed to seek different views, thoughts, and approaches. The danger in many organisations is that you get "group think", where the same team gets limited exposure to other points of view and start to think the same. A leader should strive to proactively seek out diverse thinking, both internally and from outside the organisation. I have witnessed first-hand where some of the most innovative solutions have come from people outside of the team trying to solve the problem. As a leader, the more you can enable diversity of thinking, the more you can exponentially foster innovation, creativity and problem solving.

Finally, be the shining light when it comes to creating an environment for courageous conversations.

⚒ *Practical tools*

A useful practical approach is to teach the organisation open-ended questions that create a conducive environment for constructive challenge. Suggested open-ended questions, which can be customised to your specific situation:

- Have I understood correctly, am I hearing you say xyz?

- Is everyone aligned to what I'm thinking?

- Can you help me understand your thinking?

- What factors / assumptions influenced your decision?

- That's interesting, could you explain that in more detail?

- Help me understand how that might work?

- What must prove correct for your assumptions to be valid?

- Help me understand what I may not have considered?

- Can we consider another more strategic angle?

These open-ended questions can serve as a catalyst for critically needed courageous conversations. As always, leaders go first.

Question 4.4

IS YOUR CULTURE CONDUCIVE TO EFFECTIVE DECISION-MAKING?

🔑 *Key message*

Every organisation has at some point made poor decisions which destroyed value. Very few organisations step back to ask why. The biggest root cause of poor decision-making often lies in culture. Being deliberate in shaping your culture for effective decision-making is an imperative for the protection of value and eliminating culture or process inhibitors. When decisions move past black and white, into grey areas of assumptions, unfamiliar territory, cognitive biases, or personal preferences, then decision-making becomes more open to cultural nuances. Decision-making effectiveness can be enhanced by following robust decision principles and decision-making processes.

🗨 *Key action phrase*

Create a culture of effective decision-making by following robust decision principles.

⚠ *Warning signals*

- Decision-making is often driven by the biggest ego or loudest voice in the room

- Assumptions start to become facts

- Decision-making is swayed by fact free debates

- Decision-making is disconnected to what the business outcome requires

- The organisation has a history of poor decision-making

- Decisions are counter-intuitive and not supported by the facts on the table

♀ *Observations*

In my experience value destroying decisions often emanate from a poor culture. If leaders had to honestly review those poor decisions and reflect on the warning signals above, they would most likely concur that a poor culture inhibits powerful, value adding decision-making. On the contrary, many leaders are in denial when it comes to reflecting on poor decisions. Often poor decisions are blamed on some mysterious external force, or if it is found to be internal, then excuses abound. In selected cases leaders will ask for a lesson learned review, so that they can tick the box, blame someone, and demonstrate that they took action. This is not great leadership.

Leaders need to be aware of the warning signals and instil appropriate culture checks into their decision-making process. A simple way, is to ask the following questions of culture and its impact on making robust decisions:

- Are decisions swayed by individual egos?
- Do we have assumptions that are not validated, which have become accepted facts?
- Do we have fact free debates when making decisions?
- Do we go into analysis paralysis and get derailed on minor points when making decisions?
- Do we ensure that the decision aligns to business objectives?
- Do decisions appear to be illogical?

Designing appropriate decision principles could include:

- No critical decision can be made without following the process
- When a decision falls into a grey area, set up opposing teams to defend the decision and another to oppose it. This could stress test decisions and is a powerful tool to expose fatal flaws in decision-making

- Decisions must be intuitive and rational, and easily explained. Anyone should be able to tell the story

- Note red flags or unintended consequences if the decision goes wrong, and implement suitable mitigation

- Identify triggers to pull, that can stop or reverse a decision, if things do not work out

- Create clear linkages to capital or resource allocation principles, mentioned later in question 8.4.

Deriving a robust decision-making process (expanded detail in question 10.2) entails a few simple steps:

- Asking the right question and framing the decision. What problem are we solving for and what outcome must the decision achieve?

- Establishing what minimum data is required to make an impactful decision. Data must be directionally correct

- Doing relevant analysis and testing the assumptions. Understanding what acceptable analysis is, without going so deep that you are precisely wrong

- Testing assumptions independently to the preparers and decision makers, including verifying industry context, if applicable

- Testing against existing knowledge, experienced executives, and previous lessons learned

- Verifying with subject matter experts who understand the business, context, and impacts.

The biggest warning sign for organisations when it comes to decisions is when someone has a loud voice or is very vocal about swaying the decision, there is excessive lobbying, and a decision is formulated which cannot be intuitively or rationally explained. Therefore, having an executive who is overly powerful, is a warning sign, and the organisation should be vigilant in decision-making in such circumstances.

A litmus test in any decision is quite simply – is the decision intuitive and simple to explain? You can observe many decisions that have gone wrong, and in hindsight, they quite simply were not intuitive and, in some cases, defy logic. Anyone should be able to review the decision and intuitively "get it." Your leadership decision-making success should not be left to chance, or any overly loud ego. When I reflect on one particular decision by an egotistical CEO in my construction days, it screamed out as a poor decision. My challenge was not well received and affected the relationship between us. Sadly, the negative impact of the decision was felt for years. Thankfully, I had moved onto a greater career opportunity.

Finally, effective leadership is demonstrated when everyone is aligned. If the coffee station chatter is different to the agreed decision, you may have a leadership and decision-making problem.

✖ *Practical tools*

Decisions which fall into grey areas require extra attention from leaders and the application of robust decision-making principles and processes.

Examples of decisions which could be considered to fall into grey areas:

- Debates on capital allocation for core business, growth, or innovative new business

- Employee decisions on promotions, succession plans, or discretionary incentives

- Changes in capital project assumptions, shifts in project drivers, impacts of project overruns or variations in the way projects are executed

- Changes in ways of working on core processes or systems

- Accounting matters that require judgement on the future or valuations

- Allocation of resources such as people, capital, or systems between business units within the organisation

- Any other critical business decision, where personal or cognitive biases can come into play.

Question 4.5

DO YOU EMBRACE FREQUENT EMPLOYEE ENGAGEMENT?

⚿ *Key message*

Employee engagement is a strategic leadership tool, and yet disengagement is pervasive across organisations. As a leader you should be actively engaging your employees as a key strategic priority. It is imperative that employee engagement, active dialogue, or constructive conversations are prevalent in your organisation. Effective employee engagement works in two ways, allowing you as the leader to connect with your employees, and equally it gives them an opportunity to engage you. This two way dialogue ensures that both parties are committed to mutually beneficial outcomes.

💬 *Key action phrase*

Be intentional about authentic employee engagement that embraces two-way conversations.

⚠ *Warning signals*

- You are disconnected from your employees

- You hear about critical issues from third parties after it is too late

- Your organisations employee engagement surveys indicate low engagement and even lower morale

- Your organisation has significant staff churn, and you do not know why

♀ *Observations*

Depending on which statistics you read, *circa* sixty percent of employees worldwide are either not engaged, actively disengaged, or looking for alternative employment. This is a tragic waste of human potential and energy, and an indictment of leadership. Those organisations which are intentional about authentic employee engagement have come to realise its value as a strategic lever. Imagine if you could take half of that sixty percent and turn them into actively engaged employees. This would be a significant opportunity to convert human potential into productive energy that will propel your organisation forward. This approach can be amplified by using the Liz Wiseman's Multipliers approach, which not only engages, but seeks to develop talent, cultivate new ideas and drive positive energy.

Ignoring employee engagement means that you might have your employees physically present, but many are emotionally disconnected and mentally checked out, which implies that less than half of your employees are engaged and trying to do their best work.

To be clear, employee engagement should not be about ticking a box, and the focus should be on both the actual intention and the process followed. The process should establish a fundamental platform for meaningful two-way dialogue. A few key principles should form the foundation of a robust employee engagement process, which could include:

- Transparency from leaders
- Consistency and frequency of dialogue
- Sharing relevant information that impacts employees
- Soliciting inputs, concerns, and questions
- Being open to challenge
- Providing timeous feedback
- Delivering on promises made.

The benefits of employee engagement can be exponential for morale, execution, and productivity. Effective employee engagement also means that as a leader you can quickly disseminate critical information or action required in a difficult business situation.

Employee engagement can take many forms, but a few suggestions are shown below.

- Employee surveys
- Employee check-ins
- Townhalls
- Stand-up meetings
- Focus groups or dialogue sessions
- Communications – emails or video messages
- Employee engagement platforms.

In addition to the engagement process, what is critical is what you do about it. All talk and no action simply is not a solution. Therefore, taking appropriate action is key to ensure that sustainable impact is maintained for all parties concerned.

The engagement process is one thing, but equally important is the leader's ability to communicate. John Maxwell in his book *Everyone Communicates Few Connect*[18] says, "Communicators take something complicated and make it simple." Maxwell also describes five guidelines for simplifying communication, which include:

- Talk to people, not above them
- Get to the point
- Say it over, and over, and over again
- Say it clearly
- Say less.

I love this concept of simplicity in communication, and while this may reflect my personal bias, I honestly prefer those who are short-winded in their communications. Life is too short to listen to endless waffle. However, the type of communication required is dictated by the context and circumstances. So regardless of style or duration, the fact is the leader must communicate, and not leave the organisation in a vacuum of silence.

✗ Practical tools

Earlier in my career I was appointed as one of the directors for the construction of the civil infrastructure for the Gautrain Rapid Rail project in Gauteng, South Africa. One of the first tasks given by the shareholder I was representing was to resolve the employee dissatisfaction of senior management on the project. At that time in my career, my engagement and communication styles probably left a lot to be desired. A colleague, Janet and I created an engagement and communications plan to address this challenge. The communication simply involved a bi-weekly newsletter with essential need to know information.

Some of the simple engagement tools we used

- We set up a plan to meet the top fifty leaders on the project, one-on-one and face-to-face, at their site on the project

- We created a one pager of essential information about the person, career, development areas, concerns, and often personal information. I called it my cheat-sheet, so I could meaningfully engage each person when we met

- We were deliberate in engaging about five leaders a week, thereby getting to every senior person within three months. We also encouraged them to do the same with their direct reports

- These engagement sessions shared information and it gave them opportunities to raise concerns, but most importantly it showed we cared

- We also established visible felt leadership walks every week to meet with bigger teams on site, assess safety and address issues raised.

The results were profound. We got to know everyone on a human level, we could support them when they had challenges (often family related, like sick children or ailing parents) and importantly I learned empathy. From a business perspective our South African senior leadership churn went from over thirty five percent per annum to *circa* five percent in three months.

PART 5

DRIVING TEAM EFFECTIVENESS

"A genuine leader is not a searcher for consensus
but a moulder of consensus."

Martin Luther King Jr.

Answer the following questions as accurately as possible, trusting the intuitive nature of your first response. The bonus question is intended as an outside-in view.

Part 5 – Question summary	Totally disagree	Disagree	Neutral	Agree	Fully Agree
5.1 Do you have a shared purpose that unlocks your teams' discretionary energy?					
5.2 Are you able to accurately articulate the team dynamics?					
5.3 Are you and those around you working at the right level?					
5.4 Are you deliberate in creating a collaborative working environment?					
5.5 Do you provide effective recognition for individual or team success?					
Bonus question					
5.6 Would employees unanimously agree that team effectiveness is valued?					

Once you have read this chapter, revisit your responses above and assess whether your responses remain the same.

What does this reveal to you? What three actions or goals are you going to set yourself regarding these insights?

?

Question 5.1

DO YOU HAVE A SHARED PURPOSE THAT UNLOCKS YOUR TEAMS' DISCRETIONARY ENERGY?

⌐ *Key message*

As a leader you need to create a meaningful shared purpose which articulates "why" people would want to be connected to the organisation, team, or project. Achieving alignment between shared purpose and individual purpose, encourages individuals to emotionally connect to the organisation and do meaningful and impactful work. When employees' hearts and minds are aligned to a shared purpose, they are more likely to bring discretionary energy to their work which drives greater outputs and achieves superior results.

🗩 *Key action phrase*

Shape a shared purpose, that emotionally connects the "why" for the organisation and individuals.

⚠ *Warning signals*

- Staff morale is low
- Few people can articulate the purpose and why you exist
- Teams are lacklustre and show little energy
- Staff churn is high
- Coffee room chatter is negative

♀ *Observations*

Note: Question 5.1 deals with shared purpose – why people would want to connect to the organisation or team - while question 8.1 deals with purpose – why organisations exist.

Earlier I defined discretionary effort, which implies that individuals will be emotionally connected to what they do, bring passion to their work, and use their full potential or capability to deliver their work effort.

Simon Sinek is well known for his statement of starting with the *"why"*. An organisation that is purpose-led and clear about why they exist, and can articulate it clearly, is more likely to see significant shifts in value creation for all stakeholders, including employees, customers, shareholders, society, and other influential stakeholders. Purpose defines an organisation's role to its immediate stakeholders but also to broader society. In my experience, and a broadly accepted principle, is that purpose-led organisations generally outperform those that lack a clear purpose or reason for existence.

Shared purpose is achieved when an organisation or team can articulate why they exist but simultaneously make it clear why employees, or any other stakeholder for that matter, would want to be connected to the organisation, team, or project. Ensuring that employees are emotionally connected to a shared purpose will ensure that their efforts have meaning and will ensure greater engagement and motivation. Even more powerful is if everyone can connect to the shared purpose, thereby unleashing collective discretionary energy.

Defining shared purpose should respond to a few key guidelines:

- It must explain the "why" in the context of a team
- The narrative must be clear
- It must align to individual beliefs and values that shift the mindset and attitude
- It must enable individuals to self-direct their actions, efforts, and decisions

- It must accelerate execution of mutually agreed outcomes.

I believe that this is where many organisations miss a trick. If they can be more deliberate in engaging everyone to find and connect with the shared purpose, then they can easily create a mindset shift which takes individuals from bystander to an exponential contributor. However, most organisations are wired in such a way that it is almost impossible for individuals to live the purpose and thrive within the constraints of the organisation's processes and systems.

Let me ask a simple question: Would you rather work in a place where you can fulfil your purpose and deliver a meaningful contribution to society, or would you work in a place that is inwardly focused and self-consumed? It is human nature to have an innate desire to find meaning, connect to something greater than ourselves, belong to something impactful, and make a difference. Put simply, your shared purpose must motivate leaders and employees to jump out of bed each day and eagerly serve for the collective good.

In Simon Sinek's book, *Start with Why*[19] he says, "People don't buy *what* you do, they buy *why* you do it." The same philosophy applies to unlocking talent energy. It is a lot easier to ignite the fire of passion in people when they know why they are doing something. In the absence of why, when things or circumstances change, individuals will generally struggle to adapt, because while they may understand the what, they might not understand the why.

Therefore, as a leader, it should be a primary focus to ensure that you can create a shared purpose and connect as many individuals to that shared purpose as possible. When people know why, then the possibilities for creativity, problem solving, and imagination could be endless. My experience shows that in every team or organisation, it is possible that individuals can give more energy and contribute more. Your role as a leader, is to unlock that.

✗ *Practical tools*

Many think that landing on a shared purpose is a five-minute exercise. It is not. Aligning on the handful of words that define shared purpose is hard work, but once it is defined and agreed, it is hugely impactful.

A practical way of landing on shared purpose is to facilitate a process that could include some of the following steps:

- Draw a pentagon (five sides) on a flip-chart and label the five points
  - o Customers – the recipient of whatever you do
  - o Employees – the people who will make it happen
  - o Stakeholders – those that will benefit in some way
  - o Broader Society – those who are impacted in the long-term
  - o Organisational strengths – that which gives us competitive advantage
- Ask all individuals involved to articulate the "why" from their perspective and write down two or three expressions of "why" the organisation exists (I always encourage three to six words)
- Ask them to select only one which resonates most with them
- Write (or stick or type) this into the pentagon
- Test whether each example will resonate and be fair to all five points on the pentagon above
- Start synthesizing the various versions, discarding some, changing some or agreeing some
- Through a process of refinement, finally landing on the shared purpose or *"why"* in three to six words (please don't go past ten words)
- Then stress test with others to see whether everyone can buy into it and accept it
- Once accepted by a representative group, it can be cascaded into the organisation.

The process described above can be applied for shared purpose or organisational purpose. It is also extremely powerful to use the concept of shared purpose in facilitating a leadership team, around their role either within the organisation or for a specific strategic project.

I always think that the acid test is whether everyone can personalise the "why" and interpret it in such a way that they can fully own it.

?

Question 5.2

ARE YOU ABLE TO ACCURATELY ARTICULATE THE TEAM DYNAMICS?

⊶ *Key message*

Team dynamics refers to how individuals get along, what the chemistry between them is, how they work together, how aligned they are to the goal or the team, and how functional they are. As a leader you need to sense, be aware of, read, interpret, and articulate team dynamics. It requires proactive effort to ensure that as a leader you have relevant skills and appropriate mechanisms in place to ensure that you know what's happening in your team. As with many issues a leader needs to deal with, if you can articulate the dynamic, whether good or bad, it then requires action to either leverage it or resolve the dynamic, rather than just leaving undercurrents to manifest themselves. Fostering effective team dynamics requires deliberate action, which if left unresolved, often has undesirable consequences.

💬 *Key action phrase*

Pay attention to team dynamics and proactively manage ways of working and team culture.

⚠ *Warning signals*

- You do not have a sense of what the team dynamics are
- You are aware of toxic individuals in the team, but nothing is done about it
- You have high levels of employee churn
- You are caught by surprise when issues in your team blow-up

⚲ *Observations*

Critical to team dynamics, is your awareness of them, and consequently team health. Firstly, it entails being aware of this as a key leadership activity, which should be a constant focal point. Taking a mild interest once per year during an employee survey, does not constitute awareness. Secondly, it requires cognitive mindfulness of managing ongoing team behaviours and harmony, or lack thereof. The unintended consequences of poor team dynamics are inefficiency and ineffectiveness, and by implication a significant value inhibitor.

The science around a flock of geese flying in formation, being able to fly seventy percent further through team effort, than if they were flying on their own, is familiar and has been scientifically proven. For the sake of illustration, in this book I will use the concept of the seventy percent as a directional indicator, rather than being mathematically accurate. Similarly, when I refer to minus seventy, it is a directional analogy rather than a precise calculation.

My view is that a harmonious team, as in the flock of geese, has the potential to get a similar plus seventy percent lift in outcomes, while a dysfunctional team will achieve less. When dealing with team effectiveness situations, I often ask the question, "Is this team dynamic reflective of plus seventy or minus seventy?"

Another key element of awareness is creating information flows or feedback loops on team dynamics. This can be achieved formally, (e.g., surveys or pulse checks) or informally through coffee station chats or one-on-one discussions.

Being aware of team dynamics, is only a fraction of the solution. Achieving team effectiveness requires proactive engagement, shaping ways of working, living the values, and holding individuals accountable for their behaviours. As discussed, the illustrative value, i.e., plus seventy, makes this a critical leadership activity. It is also important to point out that not resolving team dynamics will ultimately become more time consuming and costly to rectify, hence the minus seventy analogy. Getting teams to focus on positive relationships, inclusion, team well-being, and cohesive ways of working, are some focal points to get to plus seventy.

I have also often observed a sensitive issue in teams which involves what I describe as a toxic individual - someone who disrupts, drains energy and is seldom a team player, often negates team effort, and most likely drags the team performance to minus seventy. Sometimes, and obviously depending on context, you do the organisation and team a huge favour, by either removing them or transferring them somewhere else. Often, doing nothing, is quite simply not an option.

Resolving team dynamics is often complex. I often use Patrick Lencioni's[20] Five Dysfunctions of a Team model to think through complex dynamics. He describes these five dysfunctions as:

- Absence of Trust, Fear of Conflict, Lack of Commitment, Avoidance of Accountability, and Inattention to Results.

To resolve the dysfunctions, it requires deliberate actions to flip the dysfunctions around through the following actions:

- Build Trust, Engage in Conflict, Commit to Decisions, hold each other Accountable, and Focus on Achieving Collective results.

The onus is on the leader to take appropriate action to facilitate the changes and create the environment to transform the dysfunctions into outcomes that drive organisational success.

⚒ *Practical tools*

Understanding team dynamics can be relatively simple, and improvements can be achieved by spending time with teams, engaging them, listening, asking questions, and observing.

Taking action is always context specific, but Patrick Lencioni's model mentioned earlier is a useful tool. It does require some work to understand how to utilise the model effectively. I would also recommend that this type of action be externally facilitated, for greater impact.

Lastly, one useful approach I often use when facilitating teams is the following:

- I ask them to write down how they would like to be remembered for their contribution to the team

- This is normally shared with the team verbally, and then captured in written form

- Once written down, I challenge them to constantly self-reflect whether they are living up to their expectations

- I then also encourage them to start holding each other accountable against the articulated contribution.

This often leads to relatively quick shifts in behaviours and mindsets.

Question 5.3

ARE YOU AND THOSE AROUND YOU WORKING AT THE RIGHT LEVEL?

⚷ *Key message*

As you grow as a leader and move into executive roles, seldom does anyone explain what is truly required from you at executive levels. It is often assumed that you are smart, and you will figure it out. Often reality and the dream are miles apart. While many organisations give you some view of what is expected, it is often up to you, through trial and error to establish what is expected of you at your level of appointment. In the absence of such clarity, transitioning or stepping up, is often hard. Working at the right level, implies that if you are a senior executive, then do the work of a senior executive, and not that of a senior manager. This requires a deliberate focus on doing the right work, at the right level and delegating accordingly.

💬 *Key action phrase*

Create an environment where people are doing the right work at the right level.

⚠ *Warning signals*

- You are frustrated by the work of others and would rather do it yourself
- You micro-manage the work of those below you
- You believe that only you can do a job or task
- You find it easier to fix it yourself
- You do not provide feedback on poor quality work effort
- You believe that your team is not stepping up adequately

☿ *Observations*

The more senior your leadership role, the less likely that you will be told what the real role requires. This is generally not intentional, but rather a function of the busyness of senior leaders who do not take the time to tell the new person what the expectations of the role are and the level at which they should operate. Consequently, it is often left up to you, and it is often expected that if you are not doing the work required of your role in the organisation, then you should not be in the job in the first place. Great role model leaders will take the time to articulate this for incoming executives.

It frequently surprises me when I engage with newly promoted leaders, how they just cannot seem to let go of their previous jobs and related work tasks. My observation is if you are not doing the job you are allocated and not letting go of the previous role, then they do not need you in the more senior role. Having said that, stepping up can be daunting in leadership roles. It is in the interest of the organisation to have early discussions about what the role expectations are, and what you should stop doing. This simple process will save endless hours of frustration and wasted energy.

I often challenge leaders to think about what their role should be and what key stakeholders expect of them in that role. I then ask them to reflect what work they do. Often, there is a mismatch, implying that they are not performing at the right level of work for their role. The root cause is often poor delegation, or as stated before, not letting go. By delegating or letting go, it allows you to be more focused on what is expected of you and where you should be making more meaningful impact.

Not working at the right level has several negative unintended consequences. These include subordinates becoming lazy, not taking ownership for their work, and even potentially not doing their work, because they know that their boss will do the work for them. This is not beneficial to either party. In addition, a key consideration is that by not allowing subordinates to perform at the required level, you deprive them of personal growth and meaningful work.

The shift as you move up the leadership ranks is to be deliberate in taking the step up to fulfil the expectation of the next level. Previously I mentioned the four essential roles of strategic thinking, leading change, enabling execution, and driving on results. Increasingly leaders have new roles that are emerging, such as leading value creation, customer experience advocate, chief innovator, chief empathy officer, leading digital transformation, driving agility, meaning maker, storyteller, chief purpose executive, and people inspirer, to name a few.

Therefore, holding onto your old role, when there are such exciting growth opportunities and new roles to be fulfilled, seems a little crazy, well at least to me it does. Therefore, be deliberate and test regularly if you are doing what you are being paid to do.

Once you are working at the right level, it is a lot easier for those below you to work at their correct level. The positive spin-offs are mostly obvious, subordinates are given an opportunity to step-up, they can grow, they are more motivated, and they are more likely to deliver greater performance.

✖ *Practical tools*

A practical way of thinking about the levels of work is:

- Draw a series of steps with four levels
- From the top – the work of your boss, then your work, then your direct report and finally those below them
- Articulate what is required at which level
- Test with superiors in terms of expectations and what they see as outcomes from your role
- Then check how much work you are doing at the required level or below your level
- Often, a nice check is to review your diary – what have you been doing?
- Finally reflect and take corrective action.

?

Question 5.4

ARE YOU DELIBERATE IN CREATING A COLLABORATIVE WORKING ENVIRONMENT?

⊶ *Key message*

Collaboration can be defined as the action of people working together to complete a task or produce something. In most organisations, collaboration is a well-used term but often a poorly executed concept. In my experience, this is often due to culture and an environment which is not conducive to teamwork. Leaders play a key role in defining why collaboration is important, creating a collaborative environment, and establishing teams to achieve a common goal or outcome. Equally important is understanding the obstacles and organisational barriers that hold teamwork back and then removing such obstacles.

🗩 *Key action phrase*

Be intentional in creating a collaborative working environment and then structuring collaborative teams.

⚠ *Warning signals*

- The business is very siloed

- Teams do not collaborate effectively

- Effort is duplicated across the organisation, with no cohesion

- Various parts of the business compete against each other, in an unhealthy way

- Organisational KPIs tend to focus on individual effort

♀ *Observations*

Avid sports fans will resonate with the idea that achieving team success can only be achieved through collaboration and teamwork. Any discord or inability to be collaborative for the greater good of the team, often results in disappointment or even failure. The same happens in nature, such as the example of the flock of geese I mentioned earlier. Collaboration requires intent, cohesion, and effort. In the absence of collaboration, it is likely to lead to value leakage and missed opportunities.

Jeff Schwartz in his book Work Disrupted[21] says, "Today, most work is not done in functional silos but in teams or ecosystems which are networked teams connecting organisations." Given the increasing complexity of problems to solve and disruption, one functional area quite simply cannot solve for such complexity. The need for collaboration, new networks and cross-functional teams is an organisational necessity.

In the practical tools section, you will find details describing a collaborative working environment. Creating a collaborative working environment requires a leader-led shift in culture, which includes their behaviours and the tone they set at the top. If leaders do not demonstrate collaboration and it is not experienced as such by those lower down in the organisation, then executing collaboratively becomes a challenge. Coming back to the sporting analogy, if the captain talks teamwork but goes for individual glory, the results will not materialise.

My observation in organisations is that teams are often tasked to collaborate, without any clear understanding of why and what the desired outcomes are. The leader should play a critical role in defining the why, the purpose of any team, the problem being solved, the goal, or the solution required for their collaborative effort. In the absence of this shared understanding of why they are working together, it can be a challenge to expect collaboration. If the shared understanding or goal is clear, then the participants are more likely to work together and be less likely to ignore the request and revert to focusing on their own tasks or job.

The next critical ingredient is creating a collaborative environment which includes workspace, physical or virtual, ways of working, processes and tools or technology. Leaders cannot expect collaboration, but disregard the necessary tools or conditions required for effective collaboration. In the absence of a suitable environment, you get what you get, and if you do deliver, it is probably more by luck than by design. As we have seen during the pandemic, expecting collaboration virtually can be done, but quite frankly it is just not the same as being physically close, feeling and sensing human interaction. As a leader, when you want significant collaboration to happen, be intentional in driving physical proximity. It is still where some of the magic of teamwork happens.

Establishing the actual team requires intentional focus. Several considerations must be resolved: Alignment with organisational units to deliver a collaboration effort, defining roles and responsibilities clearly, not expecting members to fulfil two to three roles and finally paying attention to team composition. The latter is important to get suitable chemistry, cross-functional representation, inclusive views, and diversity of thinking. Diverse thinking is important because it creates greater value than from individuals working in isolation.

Many organisations can attest to the huge success achieved through mission-based or cross-functional teams, which are established for solving business challenges, seeking solutions, innovating, or building something new. Often the most profound questions or insights come from those who may not be involved in the intimate detail of the problem to be solved. Leaders should also be alert to natural networks and influencers in the organisation and engage them to maximise the probability of success.

I want to emphasise the expectation of having people work in two to three roles, one of which is in a collaborative team. Effort will always be diluted, and the likely outcome is probably closer to minus seventy for that individual. Individuals cannot be expected to give full energy to multiple projects or jobs. It also often leads to mental stress and burnout, and frequently it is your best talent that suffers, as they are expected to fulfil multiple roles. Often this is a key obstacle, which is something leadership can easily solve.

⚒ *Practical tools*

There are countless tools and processes for collaboration, but from a leader's perspective the following considerations could be useful in designing a collaborative work environment:

- Purpose or shared understanding – use powerful questions to frame the goal for the team

- Environment – be deliberate in creating a conducive environment both physical / virtual. With physical, you cannot expect creativity in a cramped back-office with no natural light. Design the physical space intentionally. Our new virtual world amplifies the challenge and the focus required

- Ways of working

  o Establish ground rules, decision processes, disciplines, and roles & responsibilities

  o Empower teams accordingly and create a safe environment (psychological safety)

  o Equip them for conflict management

- Team selection

  o Select people whose chemistry allows them to work in teams, although dissenting voices have their place

  o Establish rules of engagement – respect and trust

  o Cross-functional representatives, to maximise alternative views

  o Include different perspectives from different people, including external eco-system

  o Be deliberate about diversity of views

- Structural

  o Review processes and systems that will be obstacles for collaboration

  o Don't expect team members to hold down multiple jobs and deliver effectively.

?

Question 5.5

DO YOU PROVIDE EFFECTIVE RECOGNITION FOR INDIVIDUAL OR TEAM SUCCESS?

⌐ *Key message*

Recognition can be a powerful lever in driving the talent experience and is something most individual's desire. It is the appreciation or praise for work effort, behaviours, specific performance, or results achieved. The real power of recognition, besides being the right thing to do, is how it can be a catalyst for motivation, employee well-being, and improved performance. The consistent theme in this book is leader-led, so giving recognition needs to start from the top. Sometimes all it takes is showing authentic gratitude or recognising individuals and teams in front of their peers.

🗩 *Key action phrase*

Be deliberate in giving recognition for individual or team effort, great performance and successful results.

⚠ *Warning signals*

- You seldom give recognition to teams or team success
- You only provide recognition through a bonus payment
- You seldom engage teams after a successful result
- Your performance management is experienced as mediocre

⚲ *Observations*

I once spent a weekend in the Drakensberg mountains with university friends. On the menu that night were the most delicious lamb chops imaginable. After a second helping, which was just as sumptuous, I was intent on obtaining the secret to the basting sauce and asked to speak to the chef. He came out sheepishly, almost fearful. I surmised that he was only called out for complaints. I thanked him for "the best lamb chops I had tasted anywhere in the world". The diminutive chef burst into tears and shook my hand. He told me that nobody had called him out of the kitchen in twenty years. The simple gesture of recognition made all the difference to him. It made me appreciate the true power of gratitude. And yes, he did share the secret basting sauce with me, and no, mine was never as good as his. Showing gratitude can be a game changer for everyone. It certainly makes the world a happier place.

Recognition is a powerful motivator and can often enhance the employee experience in profound ways. It is important to note that recognition differs from reward, which is typically monetary or equivalent. It is human nature to seek recognition for something well done or successfully delivering an outcome. Leaders can also use recognition to create impactful value moments for individuals or teams. A "value moment" is when you leverage an interaction to create positive impact for everyone, to recognise the effort or achievement.

Some of the benefits of recognition and gratitude, and why it matters:

- It builds the organisational culture and values
- It creates greater trust and respect
- It is a powerful motivator that brings more discretionary energy
- It improves employee well-being and reduces mental stress
- It drives improved performance and productivity
- It improves the employee value proposition
- It highlights success stories
- It is likely to drive an improved customer experience.

Given the above positive outcomes, it is a leadership imperative to lead from the front and create a meaningful culture of recognition. One leader I recently spoke with sends out weekly gratitude emails on a Friday. This is a beautiful example of cultivating an improved working culture.

Think about it, lack of recognition when you have done something well, can be a serious de-motivator or deflator. A simple leadership approach is to recognise, just as you would want to be recognised for your successful efforts.

Whilst the *"why"* is obvious, the *how* is equally important. As with many leadership practices the intent must be authentic, genuine, sincere, and build the other person or team up. So, the *how* of delivering recognition is critically important and can either dial up the impact or seriously detract from it. A quote from Zig Ziglar on the topic states, "You never know when a moment and a few sincere words can have an impact on life."

Next the *"what"* of recognition must consider such aspects as the context, the nature of that which is being recognised, appropriate to the effort or outcome, it must correlate to the results achieved, and be timeous. On this last point, the timing should be as close as possible to the actual event, thereby amplifying its impact.

Finally, *who* gives the recognition is vitally important. Depending on the recognition, leaders should be deliberate in shaping who does it, which could imply that it could come from the leader, the board, peers, team members or external eco-system partners. Note, the leader is not necessarily the most effective source of recognition. My experience is that if recognition is more broadly based, then the impact can be greater, especially peer to peer recognition.

🛠 *Practical tools*

Below are a few examples of recognition principles and practices which I have used, observed, or experienced:

- Create a culture of recognition
- Make gratitude a core value
- Say thank you, and mean it
- Time the recognition as close to the action as possible
- Leaders must lead from the top
- Encourage peer recognition and nominations

- Have a platform that makes recognition easy
- Sincerity, authenticity, and sensitivity are essential
- Recognise success or milestones publicly
- Acknowledge effort, energy, commitment, or behaviours
- Celebrate successful moments that matter
- Design appropriate rewards that show appreciation
- Engage and let employees play a major role in the "what" and "how" of recognition practices.

PART 6

UNLOCKING TALENT POTENTIAL

"The mediocre teacher tells. The good teacher explains. The superior teacher demonstrates. The great teacher inspires."

William Arthur Ward

Answer the following questions as accurately as possible, trusting the intuitive nature of your first response. The bonus question is intended as an outside-in view.

Part 6 – Question summary	Totally disagree	Disagree	Neutral	Agree	Fully Agree
6.1 Are you a catalyst in creating an environment that seeks to unlock people's full potential?					
6.2 Do you actively seek to find and grow people's passion and strengths?					
6.3 Do you openly encourage curiosity, innovation, and experiential learning in the workplace?					
6.4 Are you actively nurturing and developing your talent for future capabilities?					
6.5 Are you hiring the best possible talent when looking externally?					
Bonus question					
6.6 Is your organisation seen externally as one which grows talent and fosters potential?					

Once you have read this chapter, revisit your responses above and assess whether your responses remain the same.

What does this reveal to you? What three actions or goals are you going to set yourself regarding these insights?

?

Question 6.1

ARE YOU A CATALYST IN CREATING AN ENVIRONMENT THAT SEEKS TO UNLOCK PEOPLE'S FULL POTENTIAL?

☞ *Key message*

When you reflect on what makes a business successful, there are two fundamentals which you cannot escape, you need customers who want to do business with you, and you need talented employees to produce goods and services which the customers consume or need. As a leader you have an obligation to create an environment where people can flourish, bring their best effort, dedicate energy, and potential to your organisation, which by implication drives exceptional performance for your organisation. The environment must also support overall employee well-being. If you do not foster your talent's full potential and look after their well-being, rest assured, they will go elsewhere, which will be your loss.

💬 *Key action phrase*

Be deliberate in creating an environment where *every* individual can grow and achieve their full potential.

⚠ *Warning signals*

- The organisation has significant churn of top talent

- The organisation does not encourage or seek innovation

- Leaders must drop down a level to get work done

- Performance management is a nuisance

- You have lots of bureaucratic administration

⚲ *Observations*

We have all observed and experienced situations where some of the best talent leaves the organisation to find greener pastures. Whilst it is sometimes for more money, global mobility, life balance, or other personal reasons, in most cases, they leave your organisation because you did not create an environment conducive to them reaching their full potential. While this is often caused by the organisation, it is most often also attributable to their direct manager. When your top talent leaves, despite your investment in them, they leave because the environment was poorly managed. What a waste, for everyone concerned!

My view is that talented individuals, are without a doubt the only real asset you have. Everything else has a myriad of factors you cannot really control, such as macro factors, customer decisions, or competitor moves. Your talent will either drive your success or accelerate its decline.

My experience is that it starts with the tone at the top, and how you create the emotional connection or psychological safety, that enables and gears your environment towards success. Importantly, this has nothing to do with whether the organisational leader thinks it is conducive or not. It has everything to do with what your talent feels, thinks, and experiences. Let's be honest, would you prefer to work somewhere where you can excel, be given opportunities and reach your full potential, or would you work somewhere where you are restricted and limited in what you can do?

Only if the environment is conducive, will individuals bring their curiosity, creativity, energy, courage, and imagination to your organisation, its customers, and other stakeholders.

My observation is that allowing mistakes to be made is vital. Often the best teachable moments occur when mistakes have been made. If your organisational culture is one that punishes mistakes, you will destroy value in the long run. Allowing people to learn and bounce back, will build resilience, and allow them to truly achieve their full potential. We all make mistakes. The question is how can we create a culture that learns from those mistakes?

The onus is on leadership to create an environment where people can flourish. This means thinking through many of the aspects covered in this book, including but not limited to, purpose, values, leadership behaviours, culture, well-being, workplace, policies, processes, collaboration, employee value proposition, ways of working, tools, systems, and management styles. Each requires a deliberate effort to ensure that they create an environment where people can reach their full potential. Obviously, the soft cultural issues are extremely important, but amongst the physical factors, the workplace is probably the most important. If you want people to innovate and build an amazing organisation, you cannot expect them to thrive in a dingy workspace.

As a leader you simply must be the catalyst for creating a conducive environment for success, as the success of your organisation depends on getting this right.

🛠 *Practical tools*

Creating a conducive environment for success, entails thinking through each of the elements below, many of which have been covered elsewhere in the book.

- Leadership behaviours – what behaviours are required?
- Management style – what should the management style be?
- Culture: what should the culture look like?
- Psychological safety: is it OK to fail or admit mistakes?
- Well-being: how should we bring in holistic well-being?
- Workplace: what should the physical workspace look like?
- Policies: are our policies supportive?
- Processes: do our processes hold us back?
- Collaboration: have we defined and paved the way for collaboration?
- Employee value proposition: does this support the work environment?
- Ways of working: are these clear and support work itself?
- Tools: have we provided tools required to do the job?
- Systems: are systems supportive or do they limit us?

Importantly, do not forget the coffee. Many studies have shown that providing quality coffee and suitable areas to connect in, drives productivity. Hopefully, not too many will argue against good coffee!

?

Question 6.2

DO YOU ACTIVELY SEEK TO FIND AND GROW PEOPLE'S PASSION AND STRENGTHS?

⊶ *Key message*

The path of least resistance to employee effectiveness is to harness their strengths and have them focus on what they are great at, and passionate about. Leaders therefore need to be deliberate in thinking about what work needs to get done, and who the best people are to complete that work. Matching these two elements will lead to more productive work and exponential outcomes. Performance management should also be heavily weighted in favour of building strengths and developing greatness, rather than dwelling on weaknesses.

🗩 *Key action phrase*

Be deliberate in seeking and growing individual strengths and areas of passion.

⚠ *Warning signals*

- You ignore what employees are passionate about
- Your performance management focuses on negatives and development areas
- You do not know what your direct reports aspirations are
- Your employees have limited growth opportunities

⚲ *Observations*

It is always interesting to observe how organisations tend to limit what people do or place them in roles based on organisational needs. What is often ignored is whether the individual has strengths and capabilities linked to that need, and whether the individual is passionate about that type of work. Obviously, everyone cannot only do what they are strong at and passionate about, but if carefully considered, it could lead to quantum productivity shifts and outcomes.

In the book, *The Extraordinary Leader*,[22] the authors refer to the COP model, which describes three circles, namely, Competence, Organisational Needs and Passions. The more these three circles intersect, the greater the sweet spot, and by implication the more the individual and organisation benefits. While the authors talk of competency, my view is that also focusing on strengths, improves the potential outcomes for all. Although the differences are subtle, I feel that the language is important, as it adds to the overall growth narrative when it comes to top talent.

Being deliberate in aligning organisational needs, individual strengths, and areas of passion, will lead to increased engagement, motivation, energy, and outputs. I have observed several situations where an individual was incorrectly tasked to perform work where there was an obvious mismatch across the three COP model elements. They become so demotivated that they either leave or get performance managed out of the business. I have also seen, that where wise leadership takes decisive action with the same individual and creates greater alignment, that the same individual can go from poor performance to exceptional performance, sometimes in a matter of weeks.

Leaders should be quite vigilant in understanding how individuals are positioned to deliver on work requirements or to get key tasks done. A sporting analogy could be taking a rugby forward and expecting them to excel as a backline player. You simply won't get the results you desire. The same applies in business, where you need to position the best workers with the job to be done. When I facilitate interventions for senior executives, I do an exercise which starts to reveal either the intersect or mismatch of individuals, within the team context. Whilst the exercise is simple, it is often very enlightening and facilitates much needed action.

Furthermore, leaders need to be on the lookout for what individuals are passionate about. Quite simply, if someone is doing what they are passionate about, they are more likely to deliver exponential results. As obvious as this is, I challenge you as a leader, do you know what each direct report is passionate about? If not, then you are missing out on a natural lever for success. Another critical factor is attitude. This often speaks volumes about an individual.

This leads to the related topic of performance management. I have been on the receiving end of countless performance discussions that immediately focus on development areas or perceived weaknesses, and completely ignore areas of strength, let alone passion. In my work with senior leaders, they are mostly brilliant at what they do, so that is what they should build on. In many cases, my reckoning would be that great performance is ninety to ninety-five percent strengths, and only five percent weaknesses or development areas. Why then in performance discussions would you weigh the conversation so heavily towards weaknesses? I personally always found this massively demotivating.

Having said this, you absolutely must focus on development areas and blind spots. It would be naïve to imply that you should ignore that. Addressing a development need or a blind spot in your leadership style, will ultimately increase overall effectiveness. So, this cannot be ignored.

The point is by favouring the discussion to strengths and areas of passion, you focus predominantly on what motivates an individual and enhancing these aspects, significantly increases potential and effectiveness. In your next performance discussion with a staff member, dial up the positive, and dial down the negative. You may be pleasantly surprised.

As a leader, you have a choice, unlock passion and potential, or stifle energy and effort.

⚒ *Practical tools*

When thinking about growing your talent:

- Draw four circles for each direct report – organisational needs, competence, strengths, and passion
- Articulate for each direct report – what should be in the four circles
- If you do not know, fill the gaps

- In your next performance discussion, focus on how you can get greater overlap of the four circles, seeking to make passion as important as any other.

This builds on the COP model I mentioned earlier from "The Extraordinary Leader."

I often meet with individuals, whether in a formal coaching or informal mentoring role, to discuss why they might be stuck in their jobs or why they are seeking something else. Often, they cannot explain what it is. A useful tool I use, is to ask them to go and write down their ideal job, and when they have completed that, then we can further the discussion. It often takes them several weeks, but when they do return, the clarity of thought is often a step change for them in their career. Most often, they are already in their ideal job, but all it takes is a tweak or two. For the minority, some serious decisions are required on career changes.

Question 6.3

DO YOU OPENLY ENCOURAGE CURIOSITY, INNOVATION, AND EXPERIENTIAL LEARNING IN THE WORKPLACE?

⌐ *Key message*

Creating an environment where curiosity, innovation and experiential learning takes place, requires leaders to go first. Unless your top leadership team has this open mindset, it is nigh on impossible for them to encourage or create a growth mind-set and learning culture. Leaders therefore need to have a growth mindset, demonstrate relevant behaviours, design the operating model, and architect the ways of working, for growth to take place. It all starts with the tone at the top and how leaders pitch up to lead the learning culture. Importantly, this also creates growth opportunities for the individual, which could support talent retention.

🗩 *Key action phrase*

Be intentional in encouraging curiosity, asking questions, innovating, and allowing teams to experiment.

⚠ *Warning signals*

- Individuals dominate discussions
- Loud ego's override others
- Questions from lower ranks are not tolerated
- Innovation does not happen in your business
- Failure is not tolerated
- Learning is not actively encouraged

☿ *Observations*

I have observed many organisations where leaders bemoan the lack of innovation, shortage of new ideas, and unwillingness of employees to learn new capabilities. In such cases, observing senior leaders in action will quickly tell you why this is the status quo.

Leadership must adopt a growth mindset, demonstrate openness to change, show adaptability, encourage questions, and listen to new ideas. Failure to do so will stifle the organisation, eventually driving its own demise. The environment you aspire to create, needs to start with the tone at the top. Leaders need to pitch up consistently, living the growth mindset they aspire to. This needs to be embedded through their leadership behaviours, in each interaction, and each value moment. Your talent must feel and experience a learning culture.

Think of a few leaders such as Elon Musk, Richard Branson, Steve Jobs, Bill Gates, and Jeff Bezos. Without debating their leadership style, think about the messaging they created in their organisations. They oozed curiosity, innovation, and experiential learning. They led from the front. As a leader, if you want similar growth, you must pitch up and act accordingly. It all starts with you!

It is then essential to design the operating model and architect the ways of working that will allow for curiosity, innovation and learning to thrive. In the absence of deliberate intent, you leave it to chance, and end up with mediocre outcomes, and limited growth. The design of the operating model needs to be deliberate to ensure that structures, processes, and systems are established to ensure a growth mindset. If your processes get in the way of innovation or generating ideas, then change the process. I have observed several examples where innovation is killed because it first requires a risk assessment or needs to follow an onerous governance process. In my experience this can often be an almost certain way to kill creativity or innovation upfront. The operating model needs to be enabling, rather than disabling. If the enabling environment is in place, then it is vital to ensure you have the right type of people, capabilities, and skills, as they will need to drive the growth and opportunities. Finally, leaders need to ensure that the ways of working, and structures allow for innovation and learning to take place.

For example, if you want to encourage a growth mindset, you need to think through some key practical considerations. Some other thoughts:

- Operating model – do you allow innovation to take place in collaborative teams, regardless of structure/business silo?
- People – do you hire people who are curious and ask powerful questions?
- Ways of working – do you allow for creative thinking time where people can experiment?
- Learning – do you encourage on the job training and experimentation?
- Employee experience – do you foster growth opportunities?
- Process – is the organisation open to changing processes that inhibit opportunities?
- System – do you have a system/technology to capture and progress innovative ideas?

As you can see from these questions, growth must be by design, which increases the likelihood of innovation and opportunity.

One concept that has always resonated with me, and is practised in several innovative organisations, is creating thinking time. As a leader, are you open to giving each employee a couple of hours a month, to be curious, innovative, creative, or learn?

✗ *Practical tools*

Leaders should reflect on whether they are personally demonstrating curiosity, innovation, and experiential learning.

- Curiosity – continuous learning, seeking new perspectives, constantly engaging thought leaders, reading widely
- Innovation – seeking new ideas, listening to alternatives views, ask powerful questions, dreaming of new possibilities, acknowledging limitations, and encouraging diverse thinking
- Experiential learning – moving beyond classroom training, embracing experiential learning, open to feedback

When last did you learn something new?

Question 6.4

ARE YOU ACTIVELY NURTURING AND DEVELOPING YOUR TALENT FOR FUTURE CAPABILITIES?

⚷ *Key message*

It is almost impossible to have a talent conversation today, and not hear words that refer to future fit capabilities, and yet, few leaders have grasped the significance of this key human capital shift in how talent is nurtured and developed. Each organisation should have a leader that considers the macro shifts in the industry, what the future capabilities might be and how people will need to be developed. Creating a learning organisation that is deliberate in building future ready capabilities, is essential to meet the requirements of the evolving talent models and enhance organisational sustainability.

🗩 *Key action phrase*

Design experiential learning that consistently equips your talent with future ready capabilities.

⚠ *Warning signals*

- Your training is focused primarily on legacy skills and classroom type training

- Your training is only focused on hard technical skills

- Your leaders cannot articulate what capabilities will be required in future

- Your training budget is a constant source of cost savings

♀ *Observations*

Every organisation has the sustainability high on the agenda, and yet when it comes to their talent and the future ready capabilities required to be sustainable, they could not be more diametrically opposed. In many organisations, learning and development is relegated to a mid-level manager who might be passionate but lacks the organisational support to deliver on this super-critical mandate. I often engage those managers, who express frustration at the lack of support for the talent agenda higher up in the organisation. Leaders, remind me – without talent, what will you achieve?

Nurturing and developing your talent for future-ready capabilities is a leadership imperative. Without motivated people and appropriate capabilities, the organisation cannot succeed in the long-term. Even more concerning, is that in many organisations people and talent, does not feature in their top strategic imperatives or their top KPIs. While this question deals primarily with the development of future ready capabilities, it is vital that leaders at executive level take ownership for nurturing their talent and developing future ready capabilities.

Shifting the talent and capability dial requires very intentional action from leadership. It requires critical thinking about industry trends and what capabilities will be required to meet those trends. We all know how some capabilities are in short supply, for example data scientists, and yet, we have all seen this coming for many years. My observation is that many organisational leaders are working in the details of the current business, and not lifting their thinking to the future. It is vital that a senior leader is dedicated to thinking about the future and what capabilities and talent models are required. This is particularly relevant if we think about the massive disruption that is all around us and the ubiquitous focus on the future of work.

Once you understand where future capabilities are going and what those skills might look like, you need to be intentional in designing learning journeys, creating experiential learning, and offering development opportunities, where these future ready capabilities and skills can be cultivated and grown.

The shift in learning philosophy and modalities is important to understand. Modern learning has seen significant shifts from programmatic classroom training to learning on the job, and from content to experiential learning. Like other topics in this book, leaders need to address talent development and learning as a fundamental design issue, rather than hoping it magically happens somewhere in Human Resources.

It is also important to recognise some of the much discussed future capabilities and skills which everyone talks about, but which most people are vague about. *Work Disrupted*[23] is a fascinating read on this topic and moves beyond technical skills to include innate human capabilities. Therefore, future capabilities could include:

- Innate human capabilities such as curiosity, innovation, imagination, intuition, or creativity

- Soft skills such as people management, coordinating, emotional intelligence, collaboration, judgement, and negotiation

- Hard skills such as complex problem solving, critical thinking and decision-making.

I have not even touched on some of the more technical aspects such as data science and technology. I would suggest it receives appropriate attention in your organisation, and a deep dive on what your organisation will do to ensure that your future capabilities remain relevant.

Finally, I think the greatest risk in thinking about talent and capabilities, is to be inwardly focused. If any leader tells you that they do not need external inputs or views on future capabilities, run a mile, as they are unlikely to be sustainable, and certainly will not be a magnet for top talent. Assuming you can figure out all the future capabilities internally only, is a serious value inhibitor.

⚒ *Practical tools*

In the section above, some examples of future capabilities are discussed, but I would suggest that leaders think through several elements of nurturing and developing talent.

- Learning culture – do you foster a learning mindset?

- Learning experience – have you designed an exciting learning experience?

- Learning modalities – have you shifted to experiential learning modalities that allow learning in the flow of work?

- Learning journeys – have you designed bespoke learning journeys that grow talent and creates growth opportunities?

- Future capabilities – are your capabilities and skills relevant, and will they remain so?

- Human capabilities – with the increasing growth in technology, are you cultivating innate human capabilities?

Another practical tool is to do a talent inventory on capabilities and skills.

- What do we have?

- What should you have?

- What will you need in future?

- What would be a nice to have, to create differentiation or innovation?

?

Question 6.5

ARE YOU HIRING THE BEST POSSIBLE TALENT WHEN LOOKING EXTERNALLY?

⌐ *Key message*

It goes without saying that promoting homegrown talent from within the organisation has important advantages. Promoting from within ensures that business understanding, culture fit, institutional knowledge, and ways of working are all in place. There will however be times when you simply must recruit externally, either for a capability gap or to infuse new thinking, capabilities, and skills into the organisation. When you must recruit externally, be intentional about hiring the best possible talent available. Also, be alert to a human bias, where we tend not to hire people smarter than ourselves.

🗩 *Key action phrase*

When recruiting externally, hire the smartest, emotionally mature, and positive mindset people you can find.

⚠ *Warning signals*

- Your recruitment philosophy is to hire more of the same

- You do not hire someone smarter than yourself

- You hire based on obsolete technical skills

- Your recruitment process is about backward looking assessments rather than forward looking capabilities

- You hire for culture fit

⚲ *Observations*

Succession discussions, grooming next generation leaders and senior leadership appointments, often bring out some of the worst leadership traits in senior leaders. This is because many leaders are loathe to promote or appoint people smarter than themselves. This harsh reality should be a wake-up call to organisations.

If the CEO or leader never appoints someone smarter than themselves, then they radically limit the human potential of the entire organisation, including its long-term sustainability. If this is you, then for the sake of the organisation's future success, you should probably step aside! Whilst this may seem harsh, you limit growth, innovation, and potential, to your IQ and EQ. It is not possible for you to have all the answers, all the ideas and be the smartest person. Do not limit your organisation because of your own ego.

Obviously promoting from within the organisation has significant advantages as mentioned earlier. It also serves as motivation for many in the organisation and shows a commitment to the talent that resides within the business. Having said that, sometimes, promoting from within may be the wrong decision. If the context is business growth and innovation in a new area, then an internal appointment, based on the current business may well be flawed. There comes a time for different capabilities and different business or industry experience.

When these circumstances require it, for example a new capability, alternative thinking or differentiated experience, then recruit externally, and when you do go external, be *intentional* to hire the best possible talent available. This may be difficult for many leaders to do, but as a leader, your obligation is to the organisation, all stakeholders. and the sustainability of the business, to bring in talent that increases the organisational potential. In the absence of this, you are failing in your obligations to the organisation you serve.

🛠 *Practical tools*

Simply put, when you need to hire externally, hire the best possible talent. When you hire externally do so with the "end in mind" and how will this hire build, expand, and supplement your talent pool.

When I recruit, I also look for energy and attitude, which will grow the talent base. You can always teach skills, but you cannot teach energy.

PART 7
FOSTERING RELATIONSHIPS

"You are not here merely to make a living. You are here in order to enable the world to live more amply, with greater vision, with a finer spirit of hope and achievement. You are here to enrich the world, and you impoverish yourself if you forget the errand."

Woodrow Wilson

Answer the following questions as accurately as possible, trusting the intuitive nature of your first response. The bonus question is intended as an outside-in view.

Part 7 – Question summary	Totally disagree	Disagree	Neutral	Agree	Fully Agree
7.1 Do you know who your key stakeholders are and what their needs are?					
7.2 Is servant leadership a key principle in how you foster relationships?					
7.3 Do you seek to build others up and make the community a better place?					
7.4 Do you know your work colleagues at a personal level?					
7.5 Do you really know what others want to achieve in life or career?					
Bonus question					
7.6 If you started a new business would people follow you out of personal choice?					

Once you have read this chapter, revisit your responses above and assess whether your responses remain the same.

What does this reveal to you? What three actions or goals are you going to set yourself regarding these insights?

Question 7.1

DO YOU KNOW WHO YOUR KEY STAKEHOLDERS ARE AND WHAT THEIR NEEDS ARE?

⌐ *Key message*

As you move up the leadership ranks, seldom do you anticipate the complexity of managing the stakeholders above you. These are typically individuals who are key influencers in the organisation and by implication, have significant influence on your career. It is therefore critical to understand who those stakeholders are, build appropriate relationships with them, understand their needs and be clear about how you meet and manage their expectations of you in your role. For the avoidance of doubt, this is about strategic influence and not fuelling boardroom politics.

Key action phrase

Be deliberate in understanding the needs of your key stakeholders and effectively manage their expectations.

⚠ *Warning signals*

- You struggle to meet the expectations of key stakeholders
- You cannot articulate the needs of key stakeholders
- You do not make time to engage key stakeholders
- You believe that managing stakeholders is all about politics
- You feel that you can never be sure of support

☍ *Observations*

As leaders take on new roles, the focus is seldom on who the new set of key influencers and stakeholders might be. This is often unintentional and not top of mind, as the new leader focuses on the tasks required in the new role, often doing more of what they did before. A critical success factor is to have a clear understanding of the stakeholder landscape, as they are likely to be recipients of your work outputs, decisions, deliverables, and strategic choices. Delivering your role in a vacuum could have negative consequences for your efforts. In any leadership role, it is incumbent upon you to understand the stakeholder landscape, both internal and external. As you identify these stakeholders, it is also important to understand why they may have a vested interest in you and your success.

It is also important to assess the quality of your business and personal relationships. If people do not know who you are and vice-versa, then in the absence of a personal connection, it could be challenging to resolve difficult decisions or issues. If there is at least a business relationship, then being able to connect will make it easier to resolve the matter and move forward. This does not imply that everything needs to be on a best friend basis, but to effectively solve issues normally requires a human to human interaction. I chuckle how some new leaders in new roles are intimidated by a more senior title. At the end of the day, everyone is a human being, just like you and me. Do not forget that.

When discussing stakeholders with leaders, I ask, "do you know what they need?" Often leaders cannot convincingly answer the question. It is incumbent on a leader to ask the question of key stakeholders as to what their most important needs are. Unless you ask directly, you could make blind assumptions as to what they need, which could unintentionally lead to you providing them with information which they see as a waste of time, and inadvertently planting seeds of doubt in their minds, as regards your capability. Take control of this by asking upfront. It is also useful to ask your key influencers, what they see as their biggest challenges. This often provides helpful insights on their needs and if in addition to fulfilling your mandate, if you can solve their most pressing issues, then your influence will grow positively and exponentially. When you understand what they will respond to, it will be easier for communicating what is important to you.

Moving beyond understanding their needs, another critical leadership skill is that of meeting expectations. Taking it as a given that you have executed or delivered what you were required to do, your effectiveness increases when you are able to articulate what you have done and how it serves the greater strategy or business outcomes. For the avoidance of doubt, this is not sugar-coating but articulating reality. I have often facilitated complex sessions between stakeholders, where it is patently clear to me that there is a huge communication gap. One stakeholder has not clearly stated requirements and the other has not demonstrated how the requirement was met. This seems simple enough, but it is startling how often this disconnect happens, and more concerning is the cascade of wasted energy.

Another observation, which can be a step-change in effectiveness, is the art of the clarifying question. I have often witnessed or heard about the situation where a board member or executive committee member asks a particular question. The person on the receiving end, in an effort to please and meet expectations, promises to come back with the answer. The executive then mobilises a broad team and the organisation goes into a tailspin, preparing a two-hundred page report to answer the question. When the comprehensive report is proudly tabled, the recipient may shake their head in frustration, sometimes saying, "But this is not what I asked." Ouch!

To avoid this, understand their needs, ask clarifying questions, and then meet expectations. The mind boggles how often a two hundred page report could be avoided by asking a two second clarification question.

One final thought for leaders comes from an article by Douglas A. Ready,[24] which points out that building relationships across silos creates new opportunities for value and the ability to respond to them. This strengthens the idea that stronger relationships, meeting needs, and understanding expectations, will likely bring new ideas and opportunities not previously considered.

⚒ *Practical tools*

I encourage you to formulate five to six clarifying questions that could work in your context. Use the examples below but use your language and style.

Examples of clarifying questions:

- Can I clarify what you meant by xyz?

- Am I hearing you ask for xyz? Have I heard you correctly?

- I am not clear on xyz, can you clarify your expectation?

- So that I am clear on delivering xyz, can you clarify the context of your question?

It might be useful to illustrate clarifying questions with a hypothetical example. Let's assume that an executive has tabled a business plan to the Board for capex for a new product offering.

- Scenario A
    - Board member says, "This will never work. I think it requires more work."
    - Executive feels deflated and failed to ask any clarifying questions. The result is a two-hundred page report.
- Scenario B
    - Board member says, "This will never work. I think it requires more work."
    - Executive responds, "Can I clarify your statement? What did you mean when you said it would not work?
    - Board member, "Based on my experience, I am concerned that the product might not meet customer expectations for quality."
    - Executive responds, "I note your point. Please clarify what you think might be missing on quality. Also, what additional research or data would satisfy your concern?"

- o Board member, "Customers have always complained about the inadequate charging mechanism. We need research to ensure we address this"

- o Executive responds, "Thank you, now I understand. Based on the research we did, we have redesigned that component. I'll send you the executive summary. It is a vast improvement."

- o Board member, "Great, thanks. Given that insight I support the business case."

If this sounds difficult, you can always resort to the two-hundred page report option.

I love the story of one leader I worked with, who struggled with open-ended questions, and often barged in with a very closed or limiting view. I encouraged him to use these unhooking questions. He created a few of his own and stuck them onto his access card. He experimented often with his questions and became more impactful. He was subsequently promoted to CEO of another major business.

Question 7.2

IS SERVANT LEADERSHIP A KEY PRINCIPLE IN HOW YOU FOSTER RELATIONSHIPS?

⌗ *Key message*

Servant leadership as a philosophy may not resonate with all leaders. If your leadership style is to manage and bully others to get the result you want, then you may be missing a huge opportunity. Great leaders encourage willing followers, by being intentional in serving them for the greater good, meaning that leaders work for people, and not the other way around. Servant leaders support down and challenge up. When everyone in an organisation is aligned to a common purpose, and as a leader you serve others, you are more likely to unlock hearts and minds, which will enable followers to give you discretionary energy. By serving your employees and clients with authenticity and looking out for their well-being above all else, you are more likely to create exponential outcomes for all stakeholders. How do you want to be remembered?

🗫 *Key action phrase*

To be a great leader, be intentional about serving others for the collective good.

⚠ *Warning signals*

- You see relationships as a waste of time
- Your view on relationships is about you and your needs
- You bully others to get what you want
- You are more concerned about your own career, than what is good for others and the organisation

- You are the boss; workers are there to do as they are told

- You have no idea what your people need from you as their leader

℗ *Observations*

One of my favourite activities when facilitating leadership sessions, whether for individuals or teams, is to ask the question: "How would you like to be remembered as a leader?" I then ask them to write it down. Without fail, every leader writes down an answer that is positive for either the organisation or in terms of the impact that they would like to have on people. The same goes for questions about personal purpose. I therefore find it fascinating how often leaders pitch up, behave, and lead organisations with behaviours that scream the exact opposite. I have concluded that it is a personal choice you make as a leader.

I may then be challenged because I do not understand their organisation's culture. The days of narcissistic leaders and corporate bullies are fast disappearing, and I am not aware of many organisations which still advocate this leadership style. For the organisation that holds onto this leadership style and a culture of fear, my experience and personal view is that you will rapidly slide into irrelevance. On the contrary, most organisations want to grow great leaders who are impactful and serve for the greater good.

As a reminder, investors and stakeholders see great leadership as value accretive, often reflected in higher earnings multiples and valuations. If great leadership is seen as value accretive, then investing in and developing future leaders should be highly valued. This therefore makes great leadership an economic imperative. Without digressing, the importance of leaders serving the greater good cannot be over-emphasised. More importantly, serving others can be immensely fulfilling, both personally for you as a leader, and by way of the out-sized business outcomes that become possible. Life is short. Which leader would you rather work for?

Servant leadership has a few key principles or guidelines, which you can adopt or tweak to your organisation's circumstances. These include, amongst others:

- Be authentic as a leader

- Be human in all your interactions

- Seek to serve for the greater good of the organisation and all stakeholders

- Have an abundance mindset

- Give your time and energy to others

- Seek to find optimal outcomes for individuals and the organisation

- Leave everyone better off, for having met you

- Solve their challenges, which ultimately helps you

- Remove obstacles that hold the team back

- Put their well-being first

- Find the brilliance in others

- Do not use authority to get things done

- Perform small acts of kindness to show others that you care.

Put another way, if you can serve others, and in turn they serve the organisation, the compounding effect could lead to vastly improved results and outcomes. This speaks to the power of connecting the dots and unlocking an organisation's full potential.

Some leaders may be hesitant at this point, being quick to point out that this is being soft, and people will abuse you. In fact, they may strongly advise that to get results you must be hard on people. We often hear of the terms tough and tough-minded. The differences are subtle and are often confused, especially as it relates to leadership. My view is that tough implies stubborn, difficult to deal with, and not open to challenge. Tough-minded on the other hand, is being clear on expectations, and holding responsible individuals accountable for performance and results. If done with good intent, demonstrating servant leadership, while demanding performance, is far more sustainable than hierarchical top-down leadership styles which primarily focused on how employees needed to be driven to deliver business results.

If you foster relationships with a servant leadership approach, the chances are far greater that individuals will give you their best energy, input, effort, and outputs. The concept of servant leadership is well summarised by two quotes from John C. Maxwell, "People do not care how much you know until they know how much you care." The second is, "When you decide to serve others as a leader, the team's success becomes your success."

When I think of great servant leaders, names like Nelson Mandela and Mother Teresa come to mind.

How will you be remembered? What will the leadership footprint be that you leave behind?

✗ *Practical tools*

An approach to servant leadership is to reflect on the servant leadership principles referred to in the observations section above. How would you rate yourself?

Another approach is to reflect on key decisions or key moments that matter:

- What was my intent in that situation focused on serving?
- Did I do it to serve others or myself?
- How did my decision in a key moment stack up against some of the servant leadership principles?

For interested readers, there is a great article from *Maxwell Leadership* on the link below.

https://johnmaxwellteam.com/the-heart-of-leadership/

?

Question 7.3

DO YOU SEEK TO BUILD OTHERS UP AND MAKE THE COMMUNITY A BETTER PLACE?

🔑 *Key message*

Increasingly, individuals have choices about where they want to work and, more importantly, the culture they expect from an organisation. You are competing globally for the best available human talent. As a leader you need to foster an environment which builds people up and unlocks their full potential. Whilst this is often done for an individual, it is also imperative that you create a vibrant working community, a place of belonging, and an environment where people can thrive as a collective. On the contrary, an abusive culture will fail to attract the best human talent, and your ultimate results and performance will reflect this.

💬 *Key action phrase*

Be intentional in building others up and giving everyone an opportunity to shine.

⚠ *Warning signals*

- Bosses come across as condescending and often break people down
- Getting things done is challenging
- Teams and work communities are dysfunctional
- Favouritism is prevalent
- Encouragement and recognition are frowned upon
- Employee feedback shows unhappiness and discontent

♀ *Observations*

We have all heard Peter Drucker's well-known phrase "Culture eats strategy for breakfast". I have observed this first-hand in many organisations, both positively, and sadly, negatively. Increasingly, in a much more connected and networked world, how your organisation, and you, treat people, is visible to the whole world. Given the global talent opportunities and increasing mobility of top talent, you ignore the treatment of people and a conducive working environment, at your peril. Let that sink in for a moment, how you build others up is increasingly visible and people often make choices to leave your organisation on a whim.

As a leader, your greatest opportunity to deliver results is with people. I specifically use *with* versus through, implying collaboration rather than forced effort. Ask any team sports coach, and they will whole-heartedly concur. The same applies in business. As a leader, building people up, encouraging them and giving them opportunities, are key levers for unlocking talent potential. If you focus on these three points, then most people will not want to disappoint you. Yes, there will be exceptions, but that is life. By building people up and playing to their strengths, you have a far greater chance of getting extraordinary performance from individuals and teams.

One of my favourite examples of building others up comes from *The Art of Possibility*[25] which talks of the concept of giving everyone an A. "When you give an A, you find yourself speaking to people, not from a place of measuring how they stack up against your standards, but from a place of respect that gives them room to realise themselves." This is a great example of building up and believing in them before they have proven themselves. It gives everyone the opportunity to shine.

The opposite is also true, if you unintentionally focus on the negative, knock down efforts and break people down, the chances of being disappointed, ratchet up exponentially, and people will give you the under-performance you have articulated. I always ask, *how would I like to be treated*?

The sceptic will quickly point out that giving people free reign and too many opportunities, will result in mistakes and failures. The fact is we all make mistakes, and if we allow people to learn from those mistakes, we grow and develop them, and ultimately what they deliver, improves. Use every mistake as a teachable moment, to build, not to destroy. Make it safe to unpack the lesson, so that all concerned can benefit from the teaching moment.

In my first job, post articles, I recall making a mistake on a tax matter. I had a particularly tough boss, whose initial reaction to such a mistake was often harsh. Fortunately, he saw my humility, and gave me twenty-four hours to rectify my error. This was still tough, but he was prepared to let me learn from my mistake. I came back the next day, having rectified the error, and in fact identifying a tax opportunity that was ten-fold bigger than my error.

Being intentional about fostering a community and team environment is essential. No sports team has won a world cup without creating a close-knit community, where the team is recognised as an essential ingredient for success. Organisations that create these small groups that nurture community, will be well positioned to withstand negative events.

A noble objective for leaders would be to ensure that you leave every person better off than before they joined your organisation. A critical authentic value that a leader needs is care or caring for others. Without genuine care for others, building them up will be challenging. Reflect on the extent to which you demonstrate your stewardship to others and ask yourself: "How do you build others up?"

🛠 *Practical tools*

Some practical tools for building people up, which are easy to implement, could include:

- Showing empathy
- Encourage positive action
- Listen to understand
- Seek to find the positives first
- Find their strengths and work on those

- Acknowledge them for what they do well
- Give them the benefit of the doubt
- Seek out their passion
- Give them opportunities
- Recognise and appreciate effort
- Smile and be nice.

Another way of building up the collective is to use mistakes as teaching moments. In the past mistakes often called for a lesson learned session, which generally sought to find someone to blame, so that the session could be ended as quickly as possible. Why not flip this on its head and use it as a teaching moment. This could be constructed as follows:

- Set up ground rules for the session, which creates the psychological safety
- Allow the individual who made the mistake to share their experience
- Acknowledge the courage of the individual to share
- Brainstorm what the teaching is, what the lesson is for all of us
- Brainstorm how the organisation can learn from this to improve next time
- Take action to make the changes and embed new ways of working or processes.

?

Question 7.4

DO YOU KNOW YOUR WORK COLLEAGUES AT A PERSONAL LEVEL?

⌐ *Key message*

Relationships form the essence of human connection. In the absence of a meaningful relationship and at least a personal connection between individuals, it is often challenging to achieve an optimal working relationship. I am not implying that all work colleagues must be close personal friends that meet over weekends. However, I am suggesting that it is vital to know your colleagues and direct reports at a reasonable personal level. This enables a level of appreciation for each other, builds respect, and a shared understanding when things go well, or when things go wrong. This increases the ability to show empathy and collectively achieve greater things.

🗩 *Key action phrase*

Be deliberate in connecting at a personal level, to establish a cohesive working relationship, and foster an empathetic environment.

⚠ *Warning signals*

- You do not know anything about those working around you

- You have no basis on which to connect other than work

- You struggle to show empathy when something has happened to a colleague

- You see it as a sign of weakness if a colleague talks about a struggle

♀ *Observations*

When I first started out in business, work colleagues were strictly that – work colleagues. I had a clear view that work and personal friends should not mix, as this would ensure that I could drive performance when required. Well, I did not always get the results I wanted, and sometimes I got grudge effort. I would occasionally find out later, that on a day when I was particularly tough on someone, the individual's child was sick, or they had lost a loved one. Consequently, my lack of focus on at least some level of personal relationships, meant I was cold and showing apathy. Fortunately, I now know better.

The desire to connect and belong are basic human needs, and relationships form the essence of that human connection and sense of belonging. This is an essential element of Maslow's hierarchy of needs, which dates to 1943. Most people I know want to connect with others and form a social bond. Why is there this wide-spread notion that connecting on a personal level is taboo at work? Given the leadership work I do, colleagues are often surprised at how comfortable I am engaging a CEO or a Board member. I often smile, and reply, "they are human, just like you and me."

As a leader, knowing your colleagues and key employees, is vital. Again, I am not suggesting knowing their intimate details, but try to find out about family, interests, successes, bereavement, or challenging circumstances they may be facing. Being human is simply an essential leadership quality. Showing empathy at a critical moment will set you apart. Think about a time you had a challenge at home and how your boss shouted, how did you feel? Sometimes you feel like shouting back, "You just don't get it!" Take a moment, it may make an impact that matters in a critical moment of need.

Being human enables improved connection and ultimately a more beneficial working environment. Connecting on a personal level has the potential to unlock discretionary energy from people, when required. It is our role as leaders to bring humanity back into the workplace.

John Maxwell[26] has written an entire book, with a wealth of insights on the topic of connecting. A few quotes from this book that may be useful for you to ponder over as a leader:

- "Connecting is the ability to identify with people and relate to them in a way that increases your influence over them."

- "When people trust you, they will listen to you, and they will be open to being inspired."

- "Because people will not always remember what you said or what you did, but they will always remember how you made them feel!"

As you reconsider the question of professional relationships, it will do no harm if you have a human touch and show empathy. This benefits the other person and yourself. It also grows your influence and impact.

⚒ *Practical tools*

One of the most important things is to greet people first – the human connection – smile and then enquire about how they are. Do not jump straight to task first. Earlier in my career, when I was task focused, I often just got stares. When someone pointed out to me, that I was in fact rude, it was a big wake-up call. To those who challenged me, thank you for making me more human.

Then prepare a short list on key colleagues, that includes some key facts. This could include spouse name, children's names, birthday, interests, sport, favourite teams, or challenging personal circumstances. Practice asking about one aspect each time you meet the person at the coffee machine or in the elevator. You'll be surprised at the positive response you get.

?

Question 7.5

DO YOU REALLY KNOW WHAT OTHERS WANT TO ACHIEVE IN LIFE OR CAREER?

⌨ *Key message*

Understanding what individuals want to achieve in life or career is essential. Organisations have this uncanny ability to box people into pigeonholes and expect them to perform. We often even promote individuals, giving them additional responsibility, only to find that their performance is dismal and underwhelming. Leaders gain substantial insights when they engage people to really know what they want, which unlocks individual and team discretionary energy. Subordinates also benefit by growing and achieving their aspirations.

🗩 *Key action phrase*

Ensure that you have regular dialogue with key employees to understand their life and career aspirations.

⚠ *Warning signals*

- You've never discussed career aspirations with key staff
- Selected individuals continually under-perform, despite known talent
- Some individuals appear to hold back team performance
- You make unfounded assumptions on what people really want

♀ *Observations*

Reflecting on some of my previous career roles, and how management decided what was good for me, and others, I find it fascinating that organisations can be so blinded to unlocking human potential. At some point in my career, I wanted a change from being a financial executive, a role I did for *circa* twenty years of my career in industry. When I requested exposure to a more focused management role, I was often reminded, "You are a great CFO, you should stick to that". It took changing jobs to find a more fulfilling career. Thankfully, years later, I am following my passion and purpose, which is developing leaders for a better future. While I write this book, I wonder what they would say now.

In working with leaders to drive their effectiveness, the inevitable subject of team composition comes up, which includes the individual team members and the role or structure in which they find themselves. A few common observations often surface. These include an inherited structure, individuals in roles that just do not fit, individuals that drain energy, and a structure which doesn't meet the requirements of what the leader needs, or people quite simply in the wrong roles.

Two key actions that leaders need to take, include designing an optimal structure and then ensuring that the absolute best person for the job is placed in the right place in the structure. An optimal structure is achieved when it is best able to deliver on the strategic objectives or outcomes required from that team. In other words, does the structure offer the best possible chance of effective execution? If not, align the structure to drive optimal performance. Secondly, ensure that you have the best possible person for the job. This implies having someone in the role that is suitably capable, but more importantly, has the right interest, attitude, and passion for the role. I have observed in working with leaders that underperforming individuals are often the wrong fit for the role, and unintentionally, they create a toxic environment for those around them. I have a clear view on this, change or replace the person, for their own good and for the sake of the team.

Jim Collins in *Good to Great*[27] makes a simple and yet profound point, that guides leaders to get the right people on the bus, sitting in the right seats, and getting the wrong people off the bus. Simple, but massively powerful.

Coming back to the essence of this chapter, it is vital to engage with individuals about career aspirations. I have seen countless people in wrong roles, which they absolutely hate. Often the organisational culture does not allow them to speak up or nobody asked, leading to negative energy and outcomes. On the contrary, I have also seen how leaders who engage others about their aspirations and passions, changing people in roles, or simply giving someone a different focus, can lead to exponential changes in performance. Everyone wins, but often the biggest winner is the impact on the team, previously stifled, now unleashed to greater performance. Have the conversation, you may be pleasantly surprised.

It is also important to be aware of how easy a leader can label someone. This can potentially box them and be very demotivating. It is essential to be open-minded about finding the best fit for everyone. I experienced this first-hand, switching out of finance into leadership development. Many insisted I remain in my field, but it would have been the death of my passion and purpose.

I recall a discussion with a young man I was coaching, clearly miserable in his job. I asked him if he was enjoying the job. He replied that he wasn't and would rather be doing something else. I knew that he had a passion for something other than his formal training. I asked him to think about what he wanted, and what he needed to do, to enjoy work. He came back a few days later and resigned, much to the exasperation of his father. A few weeks later, he was employed as a pilot in his dream job, following his passion, travelling Africa, and loving his work. Sometimes, all it takes is the right question from a caring leader.

A final thought. Often when a crisis hits or a part of the organisation has a huge problem, the tendency is to send in your best people to resolve the issue. This could be a huge negative for your talent. My view is that you should allocate your best people to your biggest opportunities, not your biggest problems. It is the opportunity that will drive potentially greater long-term value. Rather redirect a problem solver or hire a contractor who is great at sorting out disasters and keep your best talent motivated.

⚒ *Practical tools*

Simply set aside a few minutes, at least once every six months to simply ask these questions of all key employees:

- How can you add greater value to the organisation?

- What are you passionate about?

- What do you want to achieve in your career?

- How can I help support those aspirations?

- What do you want to achieve in life?

Great leaders will take this to heart, and proactively do something about it.

PART 8
MAKING STRATEGIC CHOICES

"Leadership is the capacity to translate vision into reality."

Warren G. Bennis

Answer the following questions as accurately as possible, trusting the intuitive nature of your first response. The bonus question is intended as an outside-in view.

Part 8 – Question summary	Totally disagree	Disagree	Neutral	Agree	Fully Agree
8.1 Can all stakeholders in your organisation clearly articulate your purpose and aspirations?					
8.2 Do you drive strategic choices that are aligned with chosen outcomes?					
8.3 Can everyone consistently articulate your organisation's value proposition?					
8.4 Are your resource allocation principles clearly defined and applied?					
8.5 As leader, do you create context and own the strategic narrative?					
Bonus question					
8.6 Is it clear and intuitive to any stakeholder how you make strategic choices?					

Once you have read this chapter, revisit your responses above and assess whether your responses remain the same.

What does this reveal to you? What three actions or goals are you going to set yourself regarding these insights?

Question 8.1

CAN ALL STAKEHOLDERS IN YOUR ORGANISATION CLEARLY ARTICULATE YOUR PURPOSE AND ASPIRATIONS?

⌒ *Key message*

It is a leadership imperative to create clarity and focus on your organisational purpose and aspirations. Organisational purpose describes why your organisation exists, while aspiration defines what your organisation pursues and how success will be defined. Your role as a leader is to ensure that the purpose and aspiration are clear and intuitive, simply articulated and actively communicated to all stakeholders. Increasingly in today's world of visibility and broad activism, this becomes table stakes. Furthermore, to truly leverage purpose it needs to be aligned to, or at least compliment your organisational strengths.

🗩 *Key action phrase*

Create focus by articulating why you are in business and what success looks like.

⚠ *Warning signals*

- Your organisational purpose and aspirations are not clear and lack substance

- You are not sure why you come to work

- Your strategic objectives cannot be intuitively explained

⚲ *Observations*

Note: Question 8.1 deals with purpose – why organisations exist – while question 5.1 deals with shared purpose – why people would want to connect to the organisation or team.

Without clarity of purpose and aspiration, it becomes challenging to focus discretionary energy on what is truly important. Using a sporting analogy, if you want to win a World Cup, you simply cannot have vague goals and hope to win. The aspiration, winning the World Cup, and purpose, for example be an inspiration to millions of children, must be clear and well-articulated to resonate, and convert into successful outcomes. Furthermore, your strategy for winning the World Cup will be about driving your game plan, which should be built around your strengths. The same applies in any organisation.

Leading through purpose, gives an organisation significantly more scope to gain competitive advantage and create enhanced shared value for all stakeholders. Therefore, explaining why the organisation exists and benefits all stakeholders, is critical to direct energy and effort. Defining the purpose, ensures that through challenging times, the leader can keep the organisation and teams focused on why their efforts are important. Often purpose-led organisations have impact beyond just goods and services, they tend to have a positive impact for the greater collective good of stakeholders beyond their immediate organisation. As Howard Schultz of Starbucks fame said, "When you are surrounded by people who share a passionate commitment, around a common purpose, anything is possible."

In the context of your purpose, defining your aspiration articulates what the organisation hopes to achieve, and by implication what you as a leader need to drive towards. Your aspiration should articulate what success would look like if the organisation, and you as the leadership team, were successful in aligning and executing on your business strategy. In years gone by organisations spoke of audacious goals, which often stretched the organisation beyond what was realistic, and this brought many organisations to their knees, because the audacious goal became bigger than reality, and egotistical leaders would drive relentlessly towards that goal. Personally, I would rather support achievable aspirations that keep the organisation focused and that allow the organisation to grow sustainably. My experience is that teams are more likely to connect to achievable or stretch aspirations, than to something that is so daunting that many will give up. Striking a balance with aspirations or goals which are believable, and still ambitious, increases the probability of broader buy-in and acceptance. For the avoidance of doubt, there is a place for audacious goals, dreaming big and outsized innovation, but ensure that it is context specific. In the wrong context, audacious goals may switch many people off.

Whilst, purpose and aspiration are clearly an organisational issue, as a leader, you have a central role in ensuring that these are clear, articulated, intuitive and leads to a call for action. This is even more critical as an organisation navigates a crisis, such as the recent Covid-19 pandemic, or even the financial crisis of 2008. Purpose and aspiration enable a leader to lead and empowes the organisation to self-direct, as they have clarity on the destination, or strategic intent.

I have worked with leaders on creating a purpose, and it is fascinating to observe how a clear purpose is like a strong light which guides teams from perceived darkness. Purpose-led organisations with great leaders and clear aspirations, will outperform competitors every time.

It is also fundamental that your purpose and aspirations play to your organisational strengths. To use the sporting analogy, there is no point in setting a goal of winning the World Cup using a certain game-plan, when your strengths are in something else. Therefore, ensure you align to your strengths, thereby increasing your probability of success.

⚒ *Practical tools*

In the practical tools section of question 5.1 it addressed how to get to your shared purpose. The approach for purpose would be similar.

The next step entails articulating your aspirations. There are many approaches and tools out there, but aspirations should include a few key principles:

- Create stretch, that generates excitement
- Be realistic, so that people buy into it
- Be intuitive, so everyone can articulate it
- Be specific so that it cannot be misinterpreted
- Be measurable, so everyone can track progress towards it

- Be translatable, so people can understand how it links to their role or job.

In thinking about purpose and aspirations it is also important to consider your organisation's strengths. The greater the overlap, the more likely your chance of success. Although strengths are generally well known, it is sometimes useful to ask others for their perspective. Ask customers or your broader eco-system partners. This reduces internal bias, and often a customer or other stakeholder will give you a unique perspective.

?

Question 8.2

DO YOU DRIVE STRATEGIC CHOICES THAT ARE ALIGNED WITH CHOSEN OUTCOMES?

⌐ *Key message*

Once an organisation has clarity on its purpose and aspirations, leaders need to clarify the strategic objectives, or building blocks, required to deliver on the desired outcome. These building blocks become the strategic choices that need to be made. Leaders play a vital role in ensuring that the narrative for these strategic choices is simple, coherent and will drive focused effort. Alignment and execution improve when the narrative has a golden thread that connects everything together, from choices, objectives, aspirations to purpose. Equally important is making choices about what the organisation will not do.

🗩 *Key action phrase*

Define strategic objectives and make strategic choices that will best deliver on the organisations purpose and aspiration.

⚠ *Warning signals*

- Strategic objectives are vague and do not have a rational link to the aspiration
- Strategic objectives are not clear
- Strategic choices cannot be intuitively explained
- Strategic choices made by leaders are difficult to interpret
- Strategic choices are made which in hindsight make no sense

☝ *Observations*

We have all observed countless corporate failures, often driven by poor strategic choices, and enabled by inept leaders. In hindsight, the reasons for the failures are often blindingly obvious, and yet when the strategy was developed and executed, they were either supported by willing participants or frowned upon by others who could not fathom the rationale behind the choices. If leadership choices could be done with perfect hindsight, it would be so easy. If only.

Leaders play a vital role in ensuring a coherent alignment between outcomes, namely aspirations and strategic objectives, and actions, which include strategic initiatives and tactical plans. The greater the clarity of choices between outcomes and actions, the greater the chances of success. I have noted that leaders often do not take time to sit back and think about the causal links of strategy. Ironing out misalignment between strategic outcomes and action, enhances the likelihood of a success.

Equally important to strategy is the narrative, or the leader's ability to tell the story. Where the strategic narrative and alignment are clear, it is easier for organisations and people to take ownership and be self-directed to deliver business results. In the absence of this clarity, when things go wrong, organisations tend to be paralysed, and forward momentum is stalled.

Alignment is one thing, but making optimal choices is even more critical. Leaders are responsible and accountable to ensure that the big strategic choices are aligned to deliver agreed upon outcomes. Organisations can be faced with numerous options, all seemingly aligned, all able to meet the outcomes, but due to limited resources, cannot all be executed simultaneously. That is where the critical role of strategic choices comes into play. When all the great ideas and options are on the table, someone must make a choice. As individuals, we face making countless choices each day. In an organisational context, the leader must ensure that the choices are articulated into simple actionable language.

In addition, the more intuitive the strategic choice explanation, the more likely it is to deliver success. Leaders are strongly advised to sanity check key choices with important stakeholders, to test rationale and intuitive links to strategic objectives. My view is that this simple, yet challenging action, could have saved many corporate or project failures. Often leaders are in a hurry because of pressure from others or externally forced timelines. Sometimes it is good to slow down slightly, align, and then proceed.

We often discuss strategic choices as the things we need to do. However, a great leader is also clear about the choices of what an organisation should not do. This helps with strategic direction and reduces the temptation to divert attention and energy to activities which can derail a team. Being clear about what not to do and what to stop doing, is powerful for an organisation. Channelling energy speaks volumes for overall organisational effectiveness.

We have all seen the situation where the organisation agrees to target blue chip customers with premium products/services. It is fascinating to see how often individuals/teams will go after smaller customers with ancillary or non-core products, where prospects/likelihood of returns is smaller. Focus needs to be on the big opportunities, not the rats and mice. When it goes wrong, it is often because of the rats and mice.

Therefore, be deliberate in choices and channelling energy and effort.

⚒ *Practical tools*

This topic could be several chapters on its own, and again there are countless examples of frameworks.

Whatever your strategic choices, ensure that there is alignment (golden thread) and a consistent narrative (intuitive explanation), between:

- Purpose
- Aspirations
- Strategic objectives (building blocks)
- Value proposition
- Business plans
- Tactical plans
- People processes and ways of working
- Priorities and actions.

In question 11.1 an illustrative example of a golden thread will be shown.

Question 8.3

CAN EVERYONE CONSISTENTLY ARTICULATE YOUR ORGANISATION'S VALUE PROPOSITION?

⌨ *Key message*

Differentiating your value proposition in an increasingly global marketplace is becoming more challenging by the day. It is essential that your customer value proposition, which is your promise of how customers will experience your products and services, is clearly understood by both customers and your employees. Customers should be able to articulate the experience, how expectations are met and how their needs are fulfilled. Employees need to articulate how they deliver the customer experience and how their efforts deliver excellence, whether it is in products or services. Leaders need to constantly ensure that the value proposition is articulated, understood, relevant and delivered consistently.

💬 *Key action phrase*

Be intentional in ensuring that everyone knows what the customer value proposition is and how the experience is consistently delivered.

⚠ *Warning signals*

- Your customer value proposition is not clear or defined
- Your employees cannot link what they do to how it delivers the customer experience
- Your customer value proposition is not easily explainable
- You can't easily differentiate from your competitors

♀ *Observations*

Customers increasingly have growing options when it comes to products or services, and as competition grows, customers' choices become progressively fickle. The customer is the determinant of your products and services ultimate success, and ultimately your financial results. As an organisation, your objective is to deliver impressive customer experiences, so that their choice to remain loyal to your organisation is an obvious outcome. The opposite is also true, if you underwhelm your customer, the likelihood of them remaining loyal to your organisation dwindles rapidly.

As a leader, you need to be clear that you understand customers' requirements, expectations, challenges, and jobs to be done, so that you can ensure that your products and services meets their needs, resolves their issues, and provide solutions to their jobs to be done. All of this delivers the customer experience, and how they feel about dealing with your organisation. Importantly, every person in your organisation should be able to explain their part in executing on the customer experience. If everyone can clearly articulate the customer value proposition, then it is more likely that they can execute effectively.

The external focus on customer is obviously the key driver, but the most valuable lever you have is to ensure that your employees delight the customer and provide them with the most impactful experience they can get. The leader plays an important role, by ensuring that the entire organisational system drives the customer experience, with employees being the key mechanism to deliver the experience through products or services.

Many employees will quickly tell you that they are back-office or support employees, and do not impact the customer. This could not be further from the truth. Every single employee in your business, has either an internal or external customer focus, which cumulatively rolls up into the final customer experience. Leaders need to drive excellence in customer experience at all levels.

Therefore, every single individual in your organisation needs to understand the broader customer value proposition, and what their role is in delivering the customer experience. Some organisations do this well, while others do it woefully. I know I am stating the obvious, but it is vital that every single employee must be clear on what the value proposition is, be able to articulate it clearly, understand it, and explain how they deliver on the value proposition.

Once everyone is clear on what the value proposition is, and their role in connecting the dots across the value chain, then it needs to be driven consistently. Consistency is what will build the brand and make your offering more valuable, in the context of customer experience. The sum of those parts will ultimately deliver your value proposition and your brand promise.

As mentioned in other chapters, be cautious of only taking an internal view. Getting an external view whether from customers, suppliers or the broader eco-system is vital. It is a serious value trap when you think that your internal views can accurately articulate how someone else experiences your products or services.

✖ *Practical tools*

Defining the overall value proposition for customers could include answering a few key questions:

- What is your value proposition and how is it clearly articulated?
- Do our customers receive a great customer experience?
- How can we improve that customer experience?
- Do all our processes serve customer needs?
- Do we meet customer expectations?
- How do we ensure and build brand loyalty?
- Is everyone clear on their role in delivering the customer value proposition?
- What obstacles can we remove that make it hard for customers to work with us?

?

Question 8.4

ARE YOUR RESOURCE ALLOCATION PRINCIPLES CLEARLY DEFINED AND APPLIED?

⌧ *Key message*

Resource allocation is one of the most strategically important decisions associated with an organisation's sustainability and optimal future returns. Leaders need to steer resource allocation to ensure a healthy balance between its current business, future growth and innovating for the future. Although resource allocation is an extremely critical executive and board function, it is fascinating to observe how few organisations bring robust rigour to this business activity, instead allowing powerful business units or voices to drive or influence where resources are allocated. The principles apply equally to the allocation of human capital and financial capital.

💬 *Key action phrase*

Implement and drive clear resources allocation principles and frameworks, which balances the core business, growth, and innovation.

⚠ *Warning signals*

- Resource allocation is done haphazardly, and often to the business unit that shouts loudest

- Resource allocation is secondary to the budget process

- Resource allocation often has disappointing outcomes

- Growth capital is seldom available

♀ *Observations*

It is a great deal easier to talk about resource allocation than to execute it effectively in a complex organisational context, especially within an ever changing global environment. As with so many things in business, resource allocation boils down to critical choices in pivotal moments in the life-cycle of the organisation. In the absence of clear principles and frameworks, those critical decisions can be swayed and influenced by strong business units, siloed factions, or even vocal leaders, often leading to disastrous outcomes. In this section resource allocation can apply to both human and financial capital.

Leaders need to firstly ensure a clear link between the strategic outcomes and resource allocation, to ensure that there is no disconnect. It is pointless if your ambition is driving customer service, but your resource allocation takes you to manufacturing excellence. Whilst this sounds strange, it happens far too frequently, even in well-established and large businesses. Therefore, being able to clearly articulate how resource allocation supports meeting strategic goals is an important leadership role.

Linked to this is determining the metrics for measuring economic return on investments. Obviously, this is easier for financial capital than human capital, but without people, financial returns are elusive. Without diving into the complexity of metrics, make sure it is a *sustainable* metric for economic margin, and can accurately reflect value creation versus destruction. The essence is, are you getting the best returns over extended time periods, human or financial, for the resources under your control?

The next critical step in resource allocation is being clear about where to allocate capital and the quantum of capital which will be allocated to the current business, to future growth opportunities and towards innovating for the future. Allocating everything to the current business, will eventually lead to a decline in sustainable returns, whilst only allocating to growth will stifle the existing business, so balance is important. For example, many organisations allocate seventy percent to the current business, twenty percent to growth and ten percent to innovation. The latter is often the one that gets cut, but which often offers the greatest long-term potential. These percentages are a guideline and are obviously context, strategy, and industry dependent. Nonetheless, establishing clarity and alignment on where future resources will be allocated is important. If for example, you do not allocate talent resources to innovation, then it is likely that future innovation will be stifled.

Another crucial function for leaders, is to establish clear principles for *how* resources will be allocated, which avoid the common pitfalls in resource allocation, for example:

- Investing significant resources into a business that has negative returns in the hope of turning it around
- Resources are allocated based only on the previous year's financial results
- Resources are allocated due to an executive who has the loudest voice
- Resource allocation has no rational link to the strategic goals
- There is no clear link to the primary value drivers of the business
- Tenuous business cases have flawed assumptions
- Resources are allocated because of past success.

Therefore, establishing clear principles is essential. Selected principles for effective resource allocation could include:

- Alignment to purpose, aspirations, and strategic objectives
- Clarity on where resources will be allocated (current, growth or future/innovation)
- Clarity on how resources drive value
- Clarity on sustainable metrics being used in resource allocation
- Impact on long-term sustainability
- How resource allocation decisions are made (decision processes)
- Ability to intuitively explain resource allocation decisions
- Ways of working in the process of resource allocation and budgeting
- Adequate capability to make informed allocations.

In addition, organisations need to create clear frameworks for resource allocation that cover basic phases including:

- Principles

- Setting targets
- Building resource budgets
- Deciding on priorities
- Decision-making on projects, human capital, or businesses
- Executing the projects effectively.

Each of these is complex and has many elements to them and will not be dealt with in this book, although a few elements are shown below in the practical tools section.

To summarise, a leader can impact sustainability through allocating resources and ensuring robust principles are applied to avoid disparate usage of valuable resources in the form of people and finance.

✗ *Practical tools*

A few key steps and considerations in resource allocation planning and execution:

- Allocation principles – selected principles outlined above
- Setting targets – link to strategy, previous performance, industry trends, market opportunities and constraints
- Building resource budgets – link to business unit plans, budget estimating, aligning to strategic choices and trade-off considerations
- Deciding on priorities – prioritisation criteria, sustainable impact, risks, mitigation, and alignment to business model/portfolio
- Decision-making – in addition to the above points the actual decision-making process
- Executing on the projects – project execution, roles and responsibilities and monitoring and tracking of the portfolio
- Lessons learned review – reflecting on effectiveness of resource allocation and refining of process.

Based on what I have shared in this book, a significant differentiator is allocating resources to the development of your organisational leadership capability. If this is adequately resourced, many other value outcomes can be achieved more effectively.

Question 8.5

AS LEADER, DO YOU CREATE CONTEXT AND OWN THE STRATEGIC NARRATIVE?

⌐ *Key message*

The art of storytelling is alive and well, and you thought it was something that ended in high school. The reality is that leaders have a powerful role to play in shaping and transforming the strategic narrative in an organisation. Whether it is conveying strategic intent or creating context for changes or responding to a crisis, leaders have a critical role to play in crafting and owning the strategic narrative. This is even more important during a major disruption, crisis or when transformation is required. If you do not own the narrative, someone else will, and you may not like the way they tell the story.

🗨 *Key action phrase*

Be decisive in shaping, crafting, and owning the narrative to support your organisation's strategy.

⚠ *Warning signals*

- Things happen to your organisation that are unexplainable

- In a crisis, it takes the organisation a long time to respond

- The organisation finds it challenging to explain shifts in the business environment

- Responding to shifts in business is a challenge

- There is a need for spin doctors to rectify perceptions or convey decisions

⚲ *Observations*

Building on earlier chapters which highlighted purpose, aspirations, strategic outcomes, and strategic choices, they can all be rather meaningless, unless they are effectively communicated in such a way that drives coordinated action and which results in effective execution. Herein lies a key leadership role: that of making meaning of context, shape and craft the story, and then communicate with impact. If you did not know that story telling is a critical leadership skill, you do now.

I have observed that despite hours of effort in shaping and defining all aspects of strategy, the ability for leaders and executive teams to articulate context, seems to be an evasive skill set for many. Leaders should build proficiency in being able to link the purpose, the "why", which was discussed earlier, and bring meaning to it, so that can be translated for everyone in the organisation to comprehend. When a crisis occurs, disruption happens, new competitors enter the market, or transformative changes occurs, nearly every person is head down, absorbed in the detail and unable to make sense of it, let alone how it impacts the business. Therein lies a critical leadership skill, creating context and providing a path forward for the broader organisation.

Once leaders have defined context and understand the path forward, or what I call the building blocks, the next critical step is communicating it effectively to all stakeholders. Whatever form the communication takes, the key is to be able to convey a story that has high impact, clearly articulates the ask of everyone, and provides momentum for positive action. A leader who can communicate effectively and drive the call to action, will gain competitive advantage.

Another critical aspect is to own the narrative. How often have you observed a crisis, in which some leaders are out there immediately controlling the narrative, while in other organisations leaders are noticeable in their absence. The message is simple, you cannot afford to be missing in action when your business reputation, brand promise and strategy is at stake. You need to own the narrative, thereby allowing you to control the choices you need to make that determine the destiny and outcomes for your business. If you let someone else control the narrative, then you will have to react to whatever storyline they choose to tell.

Owning the narrative is about authentically telling the story that supports your organisation's strategy and increases the likelihood of success. The critical element around authenticity is being able to make emotional connections for those listening to your message. If the narrative is genuine and you can create a positive emotional reaction, then it is likely that your narrative will lead to success. John Kotter is quoted as saying, "Over the years I have become convinced that we learn best – and change – from hearing stories that strike a chord within us." Success is magnified if people can make an emotional connection to what you require of them.

I recently looked after a digital learning business, which had a great foundation, but quite simply there was no story. I facilitated discussions with the team, we created context, distilled the strategic intent to one page and we collectively developed the narrative. Within twelve months, the business was more visible, and the narrative more broadly accepted. The result was a doubling of the revenue in those twelve months. Narrative works.

Finally, great leaders are deliberate in gathering stories which speak of past success, but also allows them to articulate what the future could look like. These could be their own stories, or stories of success in the organisation's journey.

✗ Practical tools

Each leader will have their own personal style in communicating, but a few thoughts and considerations for storytelling and articulating the narrative, could include:

- Be authentic and real
- Keep it simple and intuitive
- Create emotional connection
- Consider starting with a powerful question (as I have done with each chapter)
- Tell them why
- Tell them what, who, when and how
- Take them on a journey from the present to the future
- Use anecdotal stories to elaborate
- Make it real and tangible
- Make it interesting
- Encourage them to action
- Tell them why, again.

PART 9

CREATING SHARED VALUE

"Management is doing things right; leadership is doing the right thing."

Peter F. Drucker

Answer the following questions as accurately as possible, trusting the intuitive nature of your first response. The bonus question is intended as an outside-in view.

Part 9 – Question summary	Totally disagree	Disagree	Neutral	Agree	Fully Agree
9.1 Do most of your strategic choices lead to sustainable value creation for all stakeholders?					
9.2 Can everyone in the organisation articulate the top five value drivers?					
9.3 Can everyone in the organisation articulate the top five value inhibitors?					
9.4 Are your incentives/ KPIs aligned to sustainable value creation, or do they destroy value?					
9.5 Can everyone in your business describe how the organisation creates value?					
Bonus question					
9.6 Would third parties agree that you actively seek to create equitable value for all stakeholders?					

171

Once you have read this chapter, revisit your responses above and assess whether your responses remain the same.

What does this reveal to you? What three actions or goals are you going to set yourself regarding these insights?

?

Question 9.1

DO MOST OF YOUR STRATEGIC CHOICES LEAD TO SUSTAINABLE VALUE CREATION FOR ALL STAKEHOLDERS?

⌐ *Key message*

Strategic choices should be robustly tested to articulate clearly how sustainable value is created for all stakeholders. There are two key considerations in this statement, namely, sustainable value and all stakeholders. Sustainable value takes a long-term view as opposed to a short-term view, implying that strategic choices should stand the test of time. All stakeholders infer every stakeholder impacted by the organisation, implying that strategic choices should not be biased or favour a particular group, but create *appropriate* shared value for all.

💬 *Key action phrase*

Critically review all strategic choices to test whether they intuitively explain how *appropriate* shared value will be sustainably created, for all stakeholders.

⚠ *Warning signals*

- Strategic choices lead to mixed results and outcomes

- Strategic choices often have negative impacts

- The value of the organisation has remained stagnant for a while

- Strategic decisions are made by a few vocal voices

- Growth has been flat

⚲ *Observations*

In the context of this question, sustainable value implies creating value over a long-term period, rather than the more global reference to sustainability, which is part of the Environment Social and Governance (ESG) debate. Creating sustainable value for all stakeholders so easily rolls off the tongues of countless executives and their stated organisational aspirations. Yet, I find it interesting to observe how few can clearly articulate how their strategic choices deliver on this aspiration. Before decisions can be made, the two ambitions need to be understood.

Sustainable value needs to be consistently delivered over a long period of time. Value is created through five primary drivers: growing profitable revenue, managing costs efficiently, utilising assets optimally, unlocking people potential and leading the organisational system effectively. Sustainable value is created when decisions balance these drivers optimally for long-term value. A key observation is that a short-term focus, for example focusing only on cost reduction, could be detrimental to long-term value, as the organisation tends to drift into a shrink mindset, and forgets how to grow or innovate to seek new opportunities for value. I have also observed countless annual strategic objectives which focus on cost reduction and asset utilisation when the greatest value potential is achieved by growing the top line and leading the organisation effectively.

"All stakeholders" explicitly implies that value must be created equitably, as is contextually appropriate to all stakeholders impacted by the organisation. Without limiting the spectrum of stakeholders, this could include customers, employees, shareholders, government, impacted communities, investors, funders, and society at large. As indicated, it needs to be contextually appropriate, or in other words, *appropriate* to their effort, support, funding, or impact. A key observation is how often key strategic decisions are made to favour one group of stakeholders, to the detriment of others. This bias, will ultimately lead to dissatisfaction from other stakeholders, leading to a disconnect, and ultimately value degradation. It should be perceived to be equitable based on fair and reasonable expectations.

My view is that the greatest risk to sustainable value is taking a short-term view to appease institutional investors who are often only interested in daily share price gains or quarterly results. Leaders should take heed and ensure that they clarify the narrative that supports sustainable value for all stakeholders. Organisations owe it to all stakeholders to make the right decisions that appropriately benefit those stakeholders over extended time periods. Having a quarterly view, in my opinion, can often be value destroying. I do however fully appreciate that there may be a need for short-term actions, such as cost reduction during challenging market circumstances.

Another useful learning moment is to reflect on the most important decisions made over the previous few years to understand what worked well, what assumptions were made at the time, and what did not work well. Where decisions failed, seeking understanding on root causes of failures, can equip leadership teams with powerful insights for future strategic choices. Having done extensive lessons learned reviews for organisations, a key observation was that decisions were not balanced and often leadership bias played a key role in value destruction. Often the biggest learning comes from how assumptions were developed and tested, or as is often the case, how assumptions were not robustly challenged.

Therefore, the acid test is sustainability, and how it might benefit all stakeholders.

✗ *Practical tools*

Throughout Part 9, I will use the key business value drivers below. I will refer to these primarily in the business context, but clearly leaders need to appreciate the value drivers, how they integrate, and the leader's role in steering execution to cohesively drive outcomes and results. Value drivers are the levers, actions or capabilities which increase the value of something over time.

A useful exercise is to map each of the key business value drivers shown below and next to each reflect on what would drive sustainability, what the key opportunities are and where the greatest risks lie.

- Growing profitable revenue
- Managing costs efficiently

- Utilising assets optimally

- Unlocking people potential

- Leading the organisational system effectively.

This often provides meaningful insights into where leadership should focus or defocus.

See table in Practical Tools under question 9.4.

Often many strategic choices and priorities, when looked at in isolation, potentially destroy value, rather than create value. A useful approach is to consider each decision and assess how it impacts each of the five business value drivers mentioned above, assess the risks of the decision in isolation and finally, look at the unintended consequences of such a decision. Once mitigated or stress tested, then make the decision.

Question 9.2

CAN EVERYONE IN THE ORGANISATION ARTICULATE THE TOP FIVE VALUE DRIVERS?

🔑 *Key message*

Leaders have a responsibility to clearly articulate the controllable value drivers in the organisation so that collective energy is channelled to driving sustainable value. Leaders need to interpret and then create common appreciation as to which drivers create value, provide insights to the trade-offs and interdependencies that lead to value creation, then which levers to pull, and when. It is extremely powerful when leaders can explain the golden thread of how a business creates value. Equally important is to provide clarity on which levers destroy value.

💬 *Key action phrase*

Create organisation-wide understanding of most of the impactful value drivers and focus work effort on those value drivers.

⚠ *Warning signals*

- The value drivers are not clear outside of the boardroom

- Business units destroy value year after year

- KPIs drive behaviour that is siloed and disconnected to the value drivers

- Cost reduction is a preferred value driver option

🔍 *Observations*

When asked about controllable value drivers, many organisations proudly display a myriad of value drivers and a complex network of KPIs which supposedly drive value. It is not uncommon in large organisations to have hundreds of KPIs or metrics. It is far more beneficial to distil the controllable value drivers to a handful of value drivers, clarifying how they cascade into the various levels of the organisation, and then executing them well. Therefore, the first departure point is establishing the value drivers that drive the greatest sustainable value.

The key overarching value drivers mentioned before need to be interpreted for the organisational context. Illustrative examples of value drivers could include:

- Growing profitable revenue – customer experience – revenue per customer
- Managing costs efficiently – operating margin – reduced wastage
- Utilising assets optimally – return on capital employed – IRR (Internal Rate of Return) on capital projects
- Unlocking people potential – employee experience – retention of top talent
- Leading the organisational system effectively – leadership capability – future fit experiential learning journeys.

To ensure success, leaders need to be able to articulate the top level value drivers and interpret what those value drivers look like at lower levels in the organisation. For example, gross margin growth at a business unit level, could be preventative maintenance at an engineering level. Next leaders need to explain trade-offs to the business. For example, if a value driver is working capital reduction at a business unit level, it is important to understand that driving stock levels too low, could impact revenue growth, through lower sales volumes, when stock is not available. Finally, leaders need to explain inter-dependencies to the business, as everything works in a system. For example, if there is a cost reduction focus across the business, it is vital to understand that a cost reduction in say quality control, could negatively impact sales because of product defects.

Finding the golden thread of which value drivers to pull and when, is extremely powerful. Creating value is an intricate balance of investing, growing, increasing, selling, shrinking, and/or decreasing. The trick is knowing which comes when, what I refer to as the golden thread of value creation. For example, in the management consultancy industry, a golden thread will be client service levels, as it should drive all efforts for the business, whether in sales, delivery processes, investment in client solutions, or upskilling talent.

Another consideration is that often value drivers can be counter-intuitive to an accepted view of a metric. Put another way, each value driver, if viewed in isolation, has a trade-off. For example, when an organisation is under pressure, two budgets that often get cut are leadership development and marketing. The cost reduction metric may view this as wasteful expenditure, and it is often easy to cut. However, these costs should be appreciated as an investment that drives top line and helps manage the organisation more effectively, the two most significant drivers of long-term sustainable value.

Understanding the value drivers is only beneficial if it can be communicated and conveyed to every single person in the organisation. If everyone is clear on what drives value, then the leader's job of aligning work effort is made a great deal easier. Clarity of those value drivers at all levels empowers employees, ensures improved decision-making, and unlocks value opportunities.

🛠 *Practical tools*

A useful exercise is to map each of the key value drivers shown below and next to each reflect on what metric would drive sustainability, what the trade-offs are and what the inter-dependencies are.

- Growing profitable revenue
- Managing costs efficiently
- Utilising assets optimally
- Unlocking people potential
- Leading the organisational system effectively.

Another useful approach is to take perceived key metrics in the organisation, and test unintended consequences. These two approaches often provide meaningful insights into where leadership should drive value or change metrics.

See table in Practical Tools under question 9.4.

Question 9.3

CAN EVERYONE IN THE ORGANISATION ARTICULATE THE TOP FIVE VALUE INHIBITORS?

☗ *Key message*

Leaders have a responsibility to create awareness of the most significant value inhibitors in the organisation so that energy is not wasted, and value is not inadvertently destroyed. Often leaders are so deeply entrenched in the business that they do not recognise the inhibitors or obstacles. A leader needs to elevate thinking to a systemic level and identify and create awareness of that what holds the business back. Then, sometimes the most profound action a leader can take, is to remove the obstacle, hindrance, or value inhibitor. This singular action can be the catalyst for forward momentum, growth, and value creation.

🗪 *Key action phrase*

Create organisation-wide awareness of the most significant value inhibitors and remove critical obstacles that hold the organisation back.

⚠ *Warning signals*

- Obstacles keep blocking progress in business

- Similar mistakes keep being made

- Previous difficult lessons are repeated

- Everyone knows there is a blockage, but nobody does anything about it

⚲ *Observations*

In many leadership conversations, I ask what holds organisations back. Often, I get blank stares, and then after some reflection and probing, leaders articulate what they believe the biggest obstacle to their business might be. I then ask why they have not removed the obstacle, only to be met with a reflective stare. My reply: "Well if it is so obvious, and you don't remove it, who will?" This can be a major ah-hah moment for leaders.

Value inhibitors are obstacles, hindrances, or blockages in an organisation. If we reflect on these, it is sometimes staggering how much energy can be wasted by an organisation in trying to circumvent, mindlessly comply with or negate the negative drag on the team, caused by a value inhibitor. Leaders need to understand these inhibitors and unpack the root causes of the inhibitors, so that appropriate corrective action can be taken. These value inhibitors can also surface in various ways, through poor behaviours, unclear ways of working, resistance to change, outdated policies, cumbersome systems, old assumptions, or counter-productive processes.

Examples of inhibitors

- Insular focus – no one else understands our business

- Leadership behaviours – driving a culture of fear, and consequently only good news surfaces

- Policies or KPIs that stifle innovation – targets are focused on shrinking the business

- Denying obvious trends – group think forces the organisation to miss obvious trends

- Resistance to change – we have always done it this way

- Organisational structure – silos prevent desperately needed collaboration to serve a customer

- Counter-productive processes – inefficiencies are prevalent throughout an end-to-end process, causing process loss or drag.

What is important is that someone needs to take a systemic view of the organisation, applying their minds to the business, or listening to a multitude of signals being emitted from the business. Signals can often come from employee surveys, discussions, coffee room chats, exit interviews, focus groups, and often from just simply listening. Once the leader understands the root cause of the inhibitor, then it is vital to create awareness for the organisation to that everyone is mindful of how they might be wasting energy.

An example of an inhibitor can be the planning and budgeting cycle in organisations. It surprises me how this process often takes up to six months in large organisations, involves countless meetings, endless iterations, infinite detail to multiple decimal places, ample engagement, and sometimes dubious final adjustments at the end. This example can often account for significant investment of senior management time, an obvious inhibitor. Almost without fail, old processes and a reluctance to change can cost an organisation millions in wasted executive time and energy. Without a systemic view, this is often difficult to recognise, and even more difficult to change. It should not be a surprise to find that six months later, budget assumptions have dramatically changed.

My experience is that most organisations can shave off at least fifty percent of the planning and budgeting time spent by management, without any substantial impact on the budget outcome. Imagine the possibilities if that fifty percent saved time could be focused on value-add, opportunities, or innovation! Building on this theme and making it practical, take ten percent of the time saved and empower every leader or manager to commit time to innovate. Imagine the possibilities!

All that remains, is the call to action. Fix, improve, remove, or stop whatever holds the organisation back. Being deliberate in doing something about value inhibitors will provide space for renewed focus on doing the right things.

⚒ *Practical tools*

A useful exercise is to map each of the key value drivers shown below and next to each reflect on what the value inhibitors are and what obstacles hold the organisation back.

- Growing profitable revenue
- Managing costs efficiently
- Utilising assets optimally
- Unlocking people potential
- Leading the organisational system effectively.

This can often provide meaningful insights into where leadership should focus or remove value inhibitors. Repeat - take action!

See table in Practical Tools under question 9.4.

?

Question 9.4

ARE YOUR INCENTIVES / KPIS ALIGNED TO SUSTAINABLE VALUE CREATION OR DO THEY DESTROY VALUE?

☞ *Key message*

When it comes to incentives and the related KPIs that result in potential bonuses, it can be a minefield of complexity, often driven by greed. Leaders need to ensure that all incentives and KPIs are aligned to delivering the strategic objectives of the organisation and driving sustainable value creation for all stakeholders. Testing the outcomes, risks, or unintended consequences of KPIs is a critical activity, that cannot be taken lightly. Whilst many KPIs in isolation appear satisfactory, unless viewed from a systemic perspective of the organisation, they can be value destroying.

💬 *Key action phrase*

Test all incentives and KPIs to ensure that they align to sustainable value creation for all stakeholders and mitigate unintended consequences.

⚠ *Warning signals*

- Incentives drive short-term behaviour
- KPIs drive behaviour that is siloed
- KPIs drive compliance, at the expense of outcomes, or process over outcomes
- KPIs lead to unintended consequences
- Abnormal behaviours show when trying to meet a KPI
- Incentives shape culture in negative ways

♀ *Observations*

Incentives can be one of the most emotive issues in an organisation and is often linked to organisational complexity and individual motives. It intrigues me how creative employees and management can become when it comes to managing outcomes linked to an incentive. I have also observed how this is often very short-term focused and value destroying, except for the recipient of the immediate incentive. To be clear, if efforts and results deserve a lucrative incentive, then this is absolutely OK. But when it is paid to the detriment of long-term sustainability, prejudice of groups, or for the unfair benefit of some, then it requires a change to the KPIs.

Leadership therefore has a critical responsibility to test all significant KPIs and incentives to ensure that they drive the true intended outcome. Testing the outcomes, risks, or unintended consequences of KPIs is simple, and yet complex at the same time. A few questions could guide the leader:

- Does the KPI support the strategic execution of objectives of the organisation?

- Does the KPI drive a sustainable (multi-year) positive impact on growth, income statement, cashflow and balance sheet?

- Does the KPI hold back or support developing leadership or talent, or future capabilities?

- Will the KPI unlock talent potential?

- Will the KPI drive opportunities and innovation?

- Does the KPI drive sustainable outcomes for all stakeholders, or is it biased towards a selected group?

- Could the KPI drive poor management behaviours or ways of working, especially in the short-term?

- Could the KPI increase risk for the organisation?

- What are the unintended consequences (negative impacts) of the KPI, if driven too far?

- Can the KPI be manipulated in ways that damage the business, or be detrimental elsewhere?

- Are the measures, data, and metrics clear?

Should a KPI lead to any of the above negative consequences or destroy value, then it should be reconsidered, counter-balanced, or possibly even removed. Leaders should consider what the consequences are of driving an isolated metric too far.

Examples of KPIs that drive the wrong behaviour or are siloed in nature, and some real examples I have observed. There are countless similar examples.

- Production volumes versus saleable product – in one case production in a major mill was incentivised for volumes, and on a particular day they celebrated a production record. Sadly, only 65% was saleable, and the rest required rework at great cost.

- Cost reduction in one area that is harmful further down the value chain – in one case, maintenance crews were cut through austerity measures, and cost reduction targets were met. Unfortunately, machine availability dropped by over 25%, resulting in a dramatic decrease in production volumes.

- Incentivising one business unit which has negative knock-on consequences elsewhere – in one case a production unit was incentivised to reduce stock in a warehouse, which they achieved in less than a month. Regrettably the inventory was transported and stockpiled in a harbour, most of which was required elsewhere, over six hundred kilometres away.

Perhaps another consideration for leaders is simplicity and alignment – simplicity in having fewer, more impactful KPIs. I have seen many of organisations which have hundreds of KPIs, sometimes making it impossible to administer and coordinate. The risk with so many metrics, is that inevitably misalignment occurs. Rather have fewer metrics and KPIs which are aligned, drive the desired outcomes, create sustainable value and which are beneficial to all.

✗ Practical tools

A useful exercise is to map each of the key value drivers shown below and next to each reflect on what the key metrics or KPIs are and what the unintended consequences might be.

- Growing profitable revenue
- Managing costs efficiently
- Utilising assets optimally
- Unlocking people potential
- Leading the organisational system effectively.

This can often provide meaningful insights into where leadership should rethink, revise or scrap metrics.

Below represents a single table which pulls together value drivers from question 9.1 through to question 9.4.

	Growing top line revenue	Managing costs efficiently	Utilising assets optimally	Unlocking talent potential	Leading the organisational system effectively
Value drivers					
Sustainability factors					
Opportunities					
Risks					
Trade-offs					
Inter-dependencies					
Inhibitors/ obstacles					
Metrics/KPIs					
KPI unintended consequences					

?

Question 9.5

CAN EVERYONE IN YOUR BUSINESS DESCRIBE HOW THE ORGANISATION CREATES VALUE?

🔑 *Key message*

We previously dealt with organisational purpose and the customer value proposition. In this context, creating sustainable value is explaining how superior value is created and what will make the organisation successful. Whilst often intuitive and relatively easy for leaders to explain, the onus is on leaders to ensure that everyone in the business can explain how this value is created and what the organisation does to be successful. Leaders then need to communicate deep into the organisation so that everyone is clear how superior value is created and how their efforts align to creating value. In the absence of this clarity, parts of the organisation will do disparate things and could destroy value.

💬 *Key action phrase*

Raise awareness about how you create sustainable value and what will make you successful. Then ensure that everyone understands their role in achieving this.

⚠ *Warning signals*

- The value proposition to customers is not widely understood

- Very few can explain why you make money, even fewer can explain how you generate cash

- Parts of the organisation seem to drive contradictory behaviour to strategic objectives

- Siloed behaviour trumps organisational requirements

- Individuals push agendas that are not mutually beneficial

♀ *Observations*

We often hear of examples of organisational failures due to the misalignment between leadership aspirations and the work delivered throughout the organisation. This frequently manifests in poor customer service and employees driven by siloed behaviour, that negatively impacts others further down the value chain. What is more telling is how often middle management are not clear on what drives profitability, cash flow, or what makes the business successful. On the contrary, everyone can tell you what does not work.

In organisations where everyone understands their role in success, the organisational synergy is more evident, and their performance and results reflect this.

Leaders therefore have a relatively simple task of creating understanding, communicating, and continuously repeating the narrative to the organisation on:

- Ensuring everyone understands the customer value proposition
- Clarifying everyone's roles and responsibilities in this regard, whether external or internal
- How sustainable value is created and how their efforts align to this
- What really matters and where energy should be prioritised
- What the value drivers and value inhibitors are
- What will make the organisation successful and how they can support this in their business unit, team, functional area or individually.

Probably two companies that stand out for me when it comes to how this practice comes to life is Southwest Airlines and Apple. Both entities have created sustained value over time through clear focus, with all employees understanding how they serve customers and how that translates into value.

In the absence of shaping and owning the narrative on how you create value, you leave it to chance, hoping that somehow, individuals and teams will figure it out for themselves. We have all seen examples of how this can negatively play out in complex organisations:

- Different parts of the organisation have their own interpretation of the customer value proposition

- Different parts of the organisation compete for the same customers, and cut margins

- Costs are duplicated in silos

- Working capital such as stock is duplicated

- Capital is deployed to similar opportunities, but neither is truly optimal

- Capabilities are duplicated in silos, but are sub-optimal

- Processes are efficient in the silo, but are poor when taken end-to-end across the business or value chain

- Management effort is wasted and replicated.

Therefore, creating awareness and alignment on how you create sustainable value, and what will make you successful is super critical. Leaders, this is a simple, and yet profoundly important role for you to play. It should be obvious to all your employees why you get the results you do.

⚒ *Practical tools*

Formulate a simple one page message which each employee can articulate, and could include items discussed previously in the book

- Strategic narrative

- Customer value proposition

- Sustainable value creation (value drivers and inhibitors)

- Narrative that explains how you create superior value

- What really matters and where energy maximises outcomes

- Define what makes your organisation successful.

PART 10

CREATING PREDICTABILITY

"Great leaders are almost always great simplifiers, who can cut through argument, debate, and doubt to offer a solution everybody can understand."

Colin Powell

Answer the following questions as accurately as possible, trusting the intuitive nature of your first response. The bonus question is intended as an outside-in view.

Part 10 – Question summary	Totally disagree	Disagree	Neutral	Agree	Fully Agree
10.1 Do you frame powerful questions that improve predictability?					
10.2 Do you have robust decision-making processes that lead to optimal decisions?					
10.3 Is your business structured to ensure transparency of unfiltered information?					
10.4 Does your performance management process deliver intended results?					
10.5 Are you collaborating and focusing efforts to solve real business challenges?					
Bonus question					
10.6 Do external companies actively seek to emulate your business practices and performance?					

Once you have read this chapter, revisit your responses above and assess whether your responses remain the same.

What does this reveal to you? What three actions or goals are you going to set yourself regarding these insights?

Question 10.1

DO YOU FRAME POWERFUL QUESTIONS THAT IMPROVE PREDICTABILITY?

⌨ *Key message*

Powerful questions change perspectives, spark creativity, ignite passion, kindle innovation, and can create paradigm shifts in mindsets. When debating a topic or issue, a powerful question is more valuable than an unstructured or aimless conversation. A powerful question can unlock endless potential or solutions to challenges. As a leader framing the question helps focus the discussion and the problem you are trying to solve. Asking a powerful question takes quality thinking, so that it has the desired impact of unlocking a team or changing the lens on an issue. A powerful question, more than any dialogue, can unlock mindsets, biases or group think. Powerful questions can create opportunities and unleash innovation.

🗫 *Key action phrase*

Spend time understanding the issue and then frame a powerful question.

⚠ *Warning signals*

- Your culture does not permit questions

- You are not open to being challenged

- You have fixed views on topics, and do not consider inputs of others

- You do not ask questions that could add value

- Asking questions is deemed to be silly

⚲ *Observations*

Many of the greatest advances in strategic thinking, innovation and growth have come from someone asking a powerful question. Imagine where we would be if someone had not asked questions that led to electricity, the internet, mobile phones, cars, air travel and of course the coffee machine.

In my discussions with leaders, it surprises me, how under-estimated the value of powerful questions is. I have also observed how in many team environments, questions that are asked are either restrictive, i.e., require a simple yes or no, or are closed in nature, i.e., designed to confirm the view of the person asking the question.

Truly powerful questions have a few key characteristics:

- Open – e.g., what are your goals?
- Probing – e.g., could you tell me more about that?
- Hypothetical – e.g., if a crisis happened, how would you respond?
- Reflective – e.g., could you tell me more about your concept?
- Explorative – e.g., if there were no limitations, how would you solve for innovation?

Moving beyond the characteristics of types of questions, the real value comes from spending quality thinking time on the challenge, problem, issue, or obstacle you wish to solve or the objective, goal, or growth that you aspire to. Only by spending time thinking through the issue, are you able to consider asking a powerful question. If no time or effort goes into asking the powerful question, then it is likely to be some derivative of a question that has previously been asked, and you will likely only get incremental thinking. Observe next time someone asks a powerful question, and how you can see the energy in a room move.

The most impactful value of powerful questions is when it requires individuals to mentally shift, create awareness, or bring a new perspective. It is always enlightening to see that "ah-ha" moment when someone has just been challenged with a question that really gets them moving, makes them uncomfortable, or gets their creative juices going. I have often seen that a powerful question rather than a statement, can be enormously influential and motivating.

Let me provide an example of something I often observe with leaders when we discuss their subordinates and performance management. It is natural for many leaders to be protective of their team, which can disguise performance in a team, certainly as perceived by others in the organisation. If I make a statement, "I think you may be protective of your team as relates to performance", the recipient of the comment is likely to be defensive and continue reflecting the protective behaviour. However, if I change it to a question, "Do you think it's possible that by protecting your team, you may be limiting their performance?", it is likely to get a very different response. Asking the latter question, forces the individual to think – hopefully – before responding.

Asking powerful questions takes practice and deliberate intent. I always encourage leaders to keep practicing, even if they mess it up the first few times. When you master the art of the question, the results, solutions, and potential outcomes could be truly mind-blowing. If you are not asking powerful questions of your team, then who is?

By way of an example, years ago I was on the board of a steel mill, and we had challenges around the collection of scrap metal. The issue related to scrap collection and processing at a central point some twenty kilometres away. The debate remained the same over a few months. Finally, I asked, "What if we moved the processing to the steel mill?" This silenced the debate as the team mulled it over. The result was a re-design of the scrap processing at the steel mill, and significant efficiencies and cost savings were achieved.

For those who are interested, Nancy Kline in *Time to Think*[28] explores what she calls incisive questions which "…is any question that removes limiting assumptions from your thinking so that you can think again." She also explains that a question allows someone to think, which is preferred to a statement which may come across as an instruction.

✗ *Practical tools*

I encourage each leader to develop their own mini-arsenal of five to six powerful questions. I have provided a few examples below.

Individual:

- What are you passionate about?
- What motivates you to get up in the morning?
- If you achieved your biggest goal, what would success and the outcome look like?
- What action will have the greatest impact and what would your first step be?
- What should you stop doing, that will free up time for you to focus on what you should be doing?

Understanding:

- Can you help me understand your thinking?
- That's interesting, could you explain that?
- Help me understand what I may not have considered?
- Can we consider another angle to this problem?
- What is the significance of that assumption?

Organisational:

- If there was no limitation on resources, how could we solve this challenge and what could the possibilities be?
- If you placed yourself in the shoes of the customer or end-user, what would you change?
- If we could wave a magic wand, what other options or actions could we consider?
- What must prove to be correct for those assumptions to be valid?
- What obstacle do we need to remove to achieve success?

Question 10.2

DO YOU HAVE ROBUST DECISION-MAKING PROCESSES THAT LEAD TO OPTIMAL DECISIONS?

⌛ *Key message*

If probed, many organisations will admit that their decision-making processes lack appropriate principles and robustness and are often difficult to explain. It goes without saying that many decisions are simple, have adequate processes and are governed by a delegation of authority and business rules. The more complex the decision, the more important it is for appropriate principles and a robust decision-making process to be established.

💬 *Key action phrase*

Implement appropriate decision-making principles and a robust decision-making process.

⚠ *Warning signals*

- It is difficult to explain why certain decisions were made

- Some decisions are made because of the loudest voice or biggest ego in the room

- In hindsight, several decisions were poor, leading to losses

- Decisions cannot be explained intuitively and require lengthy explanations

- Fact free debates sway critical decisions

♀ *Observations*

Many organisations have made disastrous decisions, which, in hindsight, were flawed, irrational and counter-intuitive, leading to tragic consequences and most often a significant destruction of stakeholder value. It is also interesting to observe that these same organisations who made poor decisions, did not spend time learning from their mistakes and establishing alternative processes to avoid similar judgement failures in future. Learning from the past is essential, but the lesson is only learnt when behaviours and processes change sustainably. This is a concept often applied in the military, where poor decisions cannot be tolerated. By learning from past decisions, organisations can avoid future heartache.

Regarding decision-making, it is essential to follow a robust process. This is even more important given the context of corporate governance and sustainability. A few key guidelines for good decisions include defining the problem statement, testing assumptions, gathering decision-making information, the actual decision-making itself and finally the narrative which is used to share the actual decision made. Below are indicative guidelines for a decision process.

- Problem statement – defining what problem the decision will solve. Asking the right question that shapes the problem statement, is worth its weight in gold. The effectiveness of the decision and the process all hangs off the clarity of the question.

- Testing assumptions – understanding the key assumptions that support the decision. I have observed countless decisions based on assumptions which are not validated, and over time even become dangerously skewed. Transparency of assumptions and openness to having them challenged is essential. The facts supporting the assumptions must be truthful and not manipulated to look good.

- Gathering decision-making information – knowing what information will support the decision. Gathering hundreds of pages of irrelevant data serves no purpose. I observed one organisation, where no decision could be made unless they had over three hundred pages of supporting schedules. One of my favourite questions when it comes to decision-making is, "Is it directionally correct or precisely wrong?"

In other words, is there so much information and extra work, that the information loses sight of the big picture and hinders or blinds the decision-making.

- Decision-making itself – agreeing how decisions are made. It is essential to have clear principles on how decisions will be made. This needs to be contextual to the decision itself, and must define the mechanism (majority, unanimous or other) by which the leadership team will make the decision. It is also important for the decision to be stress tested. Does it make sense? Leadership maturity is once again essential to ensure robust decision-making. Game playing or internal politics in decision-making should never be tolerated.

- Narrative to communicate the decision – agreeing the storyline for communicating the decision back to the organisation. If the decision cannot be intuitively and simply told, there may be a need to review the decision. In other words, is it coherent or biased?

I want to emphasise the point of being able to intuitively articulate or rationally explain a decision. If the story/narrative used to describe the decision is not logical and requires lengthy debate/explanation for all involved to understand the decision, then there could well be a flaw in either the principle applied, or the process followed. It is then likely that a poor decision will be made. The timeless expression of hogwash (or similar) baffles brains is, in my view, a key ingredient for value destruction. Next time you listen to a leader explain a decision, and you say, "what was that all about?", be concerned.

It may be worth reflecting on poor decisions in your organisation. In hindsight, were the decisions intuitive or confusing and irrational?

Decisions can make or break your organisation, so ensure that you are robust in making them. Sometimes going slightly slower is critical. Earlier I talked about decisions in a crisis that need to be made rapidly. Obviously, context is critical, but where you have time, take an extra day or week, as the consequences of poor decisions can take years to rectify.

✷ *Practical tools*

A robust decision-making process should consider the following elements (detailed descriptions as shown earlier):

- Problem statement
- Testing assumptions
- Gathering decision-making information
- Decision-making itself
- Narrative to communicate the decision

Another practical consideration is your organisation's decision-making culture. How do your decisions get made? How does it align with the warning signals and process steps defined above?

?

Question 10.3

IS YOUR BUSINESS STRUCTURED TO ENSURE TRANSPARENCY OF UNFILTERED INFORMATION?

⌥ *Key message*

In an increasingly dynamic and fast changing world, it is a strategic imperative that transparent and accurate information flows freely in an organisation, both up and down. This requires a deliberate focus on creating ways of working, processes, and structures for critical information to flow freely within your organisation. This free flow of critical information is important to allow leaders and the business time to manage a negative situation, avert a crisis or take timeous corrective action in the event of a mistake or action that could harm others, cause reputational damage, or destroy stakeholder value.

💬 *Key action phrase*

Be deliberate in creating ways of working and processes that allow for transparent information flows, both up and down the organisation.

⚠ *Warning signals*

- As leaders you are often caught by surprise by bad news
- As information flows up the organisation, it becomes more rosy and increasingly positive
- Your culture discourages bad news or only promotes a good news culture
- Corridor gossip is rife, and often malicious

♀ *Observations*

Many leaders will tell you how they struggle to get clear and transparent information to flow in their organisation, and my observation is that this is often caused by the organisation's culture or ways of working that unintentionally stifle information flow. I have often observed that a root cause is a *culture of fear* in organisations, which then causes information to be filtered as it flows up the organisation, often with disastrous ramifications. This could be reinforced by the ways of working, which actively encourage a good news culture. In other words, sort it out and don't give me bad news.

In practice, when an individual or team becomes aware of bad news, the following scenario often plays out. Because of the culture of fear, they will seek to mitigate the bad news so that there are no repercussions. When it comes to reporting the matter, it is masked to be perceived to be more positive that it actually is. This behaviour gets repeated as it goes up the line, and as the report gets summarised, the report language becomes more positive, until ultimately when it gets to leaders, there is no issue. I have seen this scenario play out often, with negative business impacts.

Taking the leader's perspective, if there is a real issue, it is more effective to deal with it immediately, rather than let it fester and become exponentially more disastrous with time. Therefore, do not let structure, egos, and a culture of fear destroy your organisation.

To remedy this, leaders need to be very deliberate in creating ways of working and processes that allow for transparent, timeous, and accurate information flows, up and down the organisation. This means that leaders need to start by being as transparent as possible with critical information flow into the business, with obvious exceptions for sensitive information. Likewise, critical information must flow upward for effective decision-making. I am not suggesting that leaders need to be inundated with tons of information, but I am advocating that they implement mechanisms for business-critical information to flow expediently when required. This is especially important when it comes to a crisis, matters of reputational importance, people related matters, or where decisions could negatively impact business results. Effective leaders ensure that clear information flow and reporting processes are embedded at all levels of the organisation.

Leaders need to be very clear about the culture they create when it comes to sharing information flow upwards and build in checks and balances that allow accurate and unfiltered business critical information to flow freely. A critical component is the tone that is set by leaders at the top. This is not only demonstrating an open culture and psychological safety, but also asking the right questions, listening intently and being in tune with business signals. In addition, being a visible leader who walks the shop floor, corridors, or operations, enhances the chances of picking up the intuitive signals of good or bad news. As you have noticed throughout this book, culture plays a crucial role in effective outcomes. As always, it starts with action from the leader.

⚒ *Practical tools*

Each leader will have their own preferred style of encouraging information flow. Below are a few considerations which may be useful:

- People/culture
    - Review the culture to see if it encourages or limits information flow
    - Visible leadership – walk-abouts, engaging, and chatting at the coffee station
    - Openness of your leadership style for feedback or allowing challenge
    - Be aware of who the true network of influencers are and stay close to them
    - Ensure you have trusted advisors, who will tell you the truth.
- Process
    - Clarity of reporting processes for specific type of business critical information
    - Encourage speed on pre-determined topics
    - Have formal groups to which information can be channelled immediately

- o   Skip levels for critical events

- o   Review/unwind consequence management when it prevents critical information flow.

Richard Branson is famous for engaging customers, employees, and others for ideas, often walking around with a notebook. This ensures that he has a direct line to insights, along with a feel for the associated emotion and impact.

?

Question 10.4

DOES YOUR PERFORMANCE MANAGEMENT PROCESS DELIVER INTENDED RESULTS?

⌐ *Key message*

Performance management, for both individuals and teams, should be designed in such a way that it seeks to encourage everyone to bring discretionary energy to the workplace, is developmental in nature, focuses on strengths, is positive in how it drives performance, and delivers optimal business performance. I believe that it starts with the correct leadership mindset, which is about unlocking continuous potential, and not only an annual retrospective process to justify a salary increase or an incentive.

💬 *Key action phrase*

Design a performance management process that is developmental, builds strengths, and has metrics that encourage optimal individual and team performance.

⚠ *Warning signals*

- Performance management system generally does not deliver intended results

- Performance management is more stick than carrot

- Performance management tends to be punitive and focused on the negative

- Performance management is focused on deficiency/negatives rather than development/strengths

- It is predominantly backward looking and only done once a year

℘ *Observations*

It is fair to say that the subject of performance management and incentives is often fraught with complexity, emotion, and regularly leads to unintended consequences. Having said that, with the right mindset, performance management has the potential to drive significant value for all employees and stakeholders, with value in its broadest sense.

In my experience, many organisations go wrong when they treat performance management as a tool to control individuals by using it as a stick at year-end, and as the opportunity to focus on the negative. Often, it is also a process which only receives attention at the end of the year, often long after the performance event has passed. Sadly, many leaders also see the process as a wasteful exercise but are obligated to get it done.

Performance management should be about how the organisation and individuals seek mutual ways to improve ways of doing things, be more effective, drive collective outcomes, leverage strengths, and remove obstacles to success. It is in the interest of the organisation to create an environment where the individual brings discretionary energy to deliver to their fullest potential, for mutual benefit.

It may be worth pausing for a moment and reflecting on the previous two paragraphs. Which more accurately describes your organisation?

Harnessing the performance management process as developmental is also a huge source of competitive advantage. I have stated before that I strongly believe that people are your most important value lever and asset. If this holds true, why not seek ways of developing that asset to its fullest potential. Organisations will go out of their way to optimise equipment utilisation or process efficiency, but seldom do the same for people. This requires a mindset shift, that performance management is about growing, shaping, encouraging, and building individuals, so that they can bring their best potential to your customers, colleagues, and the organisation itself. If your performance management is designed differently, perhaps it is time for an overhaul.

Another key ingredient for success, is consistent and regular feedback. Quite frankly, if you only do performance management annually, then you are likely to lose your best talent and your business results could potentially be underwhelming. Adopting a developmental approach requires constant engagement, nurturing, and feedback, both ways. Designing frequent check-ins with two-way dialogue is essential. The critical factor here is two-way dialogue. It is vital that developmental discussions and feedback flow both down to the employee, but also back up to the line manager or leader. This ensures that both benefit and grow from the process.

Another key point is that if an employee is struggling with a particular performance issue, then frequent check-ins can address that early and as close as possible to the actual event or behaviour. This allows the employee to take corrective action and be proactive about improvement or development. It may also avoid uncomfortable discussions months after the event.

One last consideration is that performance/development discussions should focus ninety percent on strengths and development, and only ten percent on negatives or deficiencies. Way too many performance discussions focus on the negative. There is a host of research that talks to enhancing strengths. This will far outweigh the small gaps. It goes without saying is that if there is a fatal flaw or a leadership style blind spot in the individual, then it must be flagged and dealt with.

If your focus is developmental and on strengths, you are inherently building resilience and sustainability into the business. Do not squander this value opportunity.

✖ *Practical tools*

Below are some thoughts on a developmental approach and questions for performance management:

Approach:

- Create a safe psychological space by using empathy
- Check in to see how the individual is doing

- Provide feedback and recognition on what went well

- Ask the questions below

- End by asking for feedback and how you could help the individual succeed.

Questions:

- What do you think went well?

- What are you doing well that could be amplified?

- Which strengths and passion could you harness?

- What could you develop to make yourself more impactful?

- What one development area could you consider for improvement?

- What could you stop doing that holds you back?

?

Question 10.5

ARE YOU COLLABORATING AND FOCUSING EFFORTS TO SOLVE REAL BUSINESS CHALLENGES?

⊶ *Key message*

Most complex business challenges are systemic in nature, inferring that they do not just reside in a single function or operational area. Solving these complex challenges requires a holistic view of the organisation to understand the end-to-end implications and solutions. Likewise, creating opportunities is best achieved through collaborative teams with a broad view. Therefore, the organisation needs to be deliberate in creating cross-functional teams, collaborative ways of working, processes that support working across business silos, and key performance indicators (KPIs) that recognise the value of solving systemic challenges. Collaboration happens best by design.

🗩 *Key action phrase*

Be intentional in designing collaboration to create opportunities and solve systemic business challenges.

⚠ *Warning signals*

- The organisation functions in silos
- Solving business challenges is problematic
- There is reluctance to support across business unit boundaries
- KPIs discourage participation in cross-functional teams

♀ *Observations*

Many organisations will happily indicate that they have mastered cross-functional teams to solve complex business challenges, and yet the results, processes and ways of working indicate the opposite. Sound familiar? The reality is that many organisations fail dismally at solving complex problems, and bleed resources and capital in the process. This is not for want of trying, but more from failing to design collaboration for success. Whilst this question focuses on challenges, the opposite for opportunities also holds true.

Prior to considering collaborative teams to solve complex problems, leaders need to prioritise the biggest challenges, frame the question or problem to solve, and have a view of the obstacles an organisation faces in addressing the challenge. Often, the biggest enemy is time, with leaders not having enough quality thinking time to sit back and understand issues and anticipate obstacles. This may seem clear, but many leaders are so caught up working *in* the business, that the obvious eludes them until it becomes a crisis. Therefore, clarity on goals or outcomes you want a collaborative team to achieve is essential.

Establishing cross-functional teams requires a deliberate design of ways of working, structures, processes, and systems. Existing organisational silos, priorities and KPIs often have a nasty way of countering any effort to work across functional or business boundaries. It requires intentional design and establishing mutually beneficial ways of working to solve the issue and unlock real value.

Selected considerations for establishing collaborative teams could include:

- Structure – leadership role, reporting lines, responsibilities, flat structures, diversity of thinking
- Ways of working – decision rights, voting, conflict management, communication, psychological safety, team principles (examples are included under practical tools)
- Processes – meeting processes, standards to apply, quality requirements, design thinking
- Systems – collaboration tools, technology to leverage.

Next, is to consider these challenges as opportunities to either improve the organisation or take advantage of the challenge to create new value. When you can rally the team around the opportunity or value potential, it is a lot easier to align collective efforts to solve the challenge and turn it into an advantage. Establishing the "why" for collaborative teams is essential to focus the energy of teams.

The single biggest failing I have observed is that leaders set up cross-functional teams, drawing talent from across the organisation, but still expect them to fulfil a full job elsewhere. That is why you often hear the expression, "This is great, but tonight, I will need to go back and do my day job." This is neither optimal nor fair.

One last thing, if the challenge and opportunity are significant, be conscious about putting some of your best talent onto the team.

✖ *Practical tools*

Working in collaborative teams requires some guiding principles or ways of working. These could include:

- Listen to understand
- Ask open-ended questions
- Allow all voices to be heard, even if at first an idea sounds silly
- Drop your functional or operational bias
- Adopt a customer/outside in mindset
- Allow for diverse and wide initial discussion, but then narrow it down
- When implementing start small and then scale up
- Be present and fully participate
- Allow members to dig a little deeper than normal
- Be open to challenge and feedback
- Be aware of your biases
- Challenge existing assumptions freely.

PART 11

DRIVING EFFECTIVE EXECUTION

"Effective leadership is putting first things first. Effective management is discipline, carrying it out."

Stephen Covey

Answer the following questions as accurately as possible, trusting the intuitive nature of your first response. The bonus question is intended as an outside-in view.

Part 11 – Question summary	Totally disagree	Disagree	Neutral	Agree	Fully Agree
11.1 Is there a tangible link between strategic intent and tactical execution?					
11.2 Do you consistently test end-to-end value chain execution effectiveness?					
11.3 Do you drive effectiveness through meaningful work?					
11.4 Do you focus on the right things and how well you are doing them?					
11.5 Do you run effective meetings?					
Bonus question					
11.6 Is it easy to explain why you get the results you do?					

Once you have read this chapter, revisit your responses above and assess whether your responses remain the same.

What does this reveal to you? What three actions or goals are you going to set yourself regarding these insights?

?

Question 11.1

IS THERE A TANGIBLE LINK BETWEEN STRATEGIC INTENT AND TACTICAL EXECUTION?

⌐ *Key message*

Finding the golden thread that takes strategic intent and links it to tactical execution sounds simple but is often elusive for many leaders. A critical role for leaders is to effectively cascade strategic intent into strategic objectives and then into tactical actions, which are easily understood at lower levels in the organisation. The golden thread is when all these actions are intuitively connected, to ensure that effort across the organisation is aligned to the overall strategy. The ability to focus energy on the golden threads – that which pulls it all together – is essential to driving effective execution, and maximising return on effort.

💬 *Key action phrase*

Create intuitive links between strategy, strategic objectives, and tactical execution.

⚠ *Warning signals*

- There is a disconnect between execution and what the strategic drivers are
- Lower-level managers cannot intuitively explain how their efforts drive strategy
- Mid-level managers cannot explain how their efforts deliver the strategy
- Work effort is done in silos

⚲ *Observations*

When strategic intent is translated into strategic objectives, it should have a strong link to the primary value drivers shown below.

Leaders then have a critical role to play in translating strategic intent and value drivers into strategic and tactical actions. It is then a lot easier to show what an employee should do or what skills they would require. For illustrative purposes I have shown a very simple table below reflecting these linkages.

Strategic Intent	Value driver	Strategic action	Tactical action	Employee action or skill
Organic growth	Growing top line revenue	Unique customer experience	Reconfigure customer service processes	Service excellence training
Margin improvement	Managing costs efficiently	Leverage strategic sourcing	Rationalise vendors	Analytics and negotiation skills
Capital optimisation	Utilising assets optimally	Improve plant utilisation	Plant availability and preventative maintenance	Operator effectiveness
Employer of Choice	Unlocking people potential	Enhance employee experience	Employee engagement	Engagement tool design
Leadership Capability	Managing the system effectively	Build leadership pipeline	Design learning journeys	Leadership development facilitation

Earlier I mentioned the golden thread. This is taking the employee action and easily linking that to the strategic intent. For example, showing how an employee's analytics efforts/skill contributes to margin improvement.

I will use an example of a bulk mining operation to demonstrate a slightly more integrated golden thread. In this example, the key employee focus was on supervisor and operator effectiveness. Because of focusing on the golden thread of supervisor and operator effectiveness, strategy and value drivers were positively impacted as follows:

- Growing top line revenue – improved productivity and asset availability across the system allowed for increased volumes

- Managing costs efficiently – operators adopted an owner mindset and were aware of variable expenses such as fuel usage and tyre wear and tear

- Utilising assets optimally – preventative maintenance led to improved availability, better utilization, reduced capex spend, improved machine overhauls

- Unlocking people potential – motivated operators earned better production bonuses, took less absenteeism, and innovated (haul road maintenance)

- Managing the organisational system effectively – trained supervisors had a more holistic view, engaged operators, resulting in less disruptions and down-time.

This gives you a sense of the golden thread concept. Interested readers may want to read further on value based management, which expands on this topic.

Another interesting observation is to reflect on the critical value drivers mentioned

- Often the greatest drivers of value or opportunity are growing top line revenue and leading the organisation system effectively

- These are often also the areas which have the greatest risk and opportunity

- And yet, most strategic priorities are often focused on asset optimisation or cost reduction.

When leaders are confronted with this insight, they are often surprised. This could emanate from a shrink mindset, which is sweating the assets and relentless cost reduction. Instead, it should be a growth mindset, looking for top line growth and finding smarter ways of doing things across the whole system.

The key to execution effectiveness is understanding the golden threads and which actions or levers to pull, and when.

⚒ *Practical tools*

There are a variety of frameworks and tools, both manual and digital, for unpacking value drivers and causal links, including but not limited to:

- Value driver maps

- Strategy maps

- Driver models

- Leadership value maps

It is probably most useful to consult your business to see what they have available. Your role is to ensure that the value links and the golden threads are clearly understood.

?

Question 11.2

DO YOU CONSISTENTLY TEST END-TO-END VALUE CHAIN EXECUTION EFFECTIVENESS?

⌐ *Key message*

Assessing execution effectiveness typically entails focusing on a micro level and seeking incremental changes or improvements. Driving effectiveness across the value chain sounds simple enough, but organisational complexity, business silos, and legacy structures often get in the way. Driving execution effectiveness requires a systemic approach to assess end-to-end value chain efficiency, removing constraints, seeking synergies, and optimising hand-over points. The secret is to significantly simplify wherever feasibly possible.

🗩 *Key action phrase*

Drive execution effectiveness by radically simplifying the entire value chain, hand-over points, and constraints.

⚠ *Warning signals*

- Execution efficiency in assessed in isolation or in silos

- The impact of processes is not assessed outside of their own organisational silo

- Everyone is partly aware of pain points, but no one does anything about it

- The organisation cultivates complexity

♀ *Observations*

Execution effectiveness initiatives are often pushed down into the organisation through KPIs at a functional, business unit level, or into a structural silo. While this is logical, it undoubtedly causes the organisation to seek efficiencies in a narrow and incrementally continuous improvement manner. Each manager has a KPI target and will often work in isolation to achieve that. In the absence of a more systemic end-to-end approach, execution efficiency gains could be marginal at best, and occasionally narrow cost reduction hampers effectiveness elsewhere.

Unlocking execution effectiveness requires the level of thinking to be elevated to a value chain or systemic view, and to test effectiveness across the entire value chain and system. This elevated view is more likely to find the obstacles, bottlenecks, and constraints that hold back the business, and consequently find the opportunity to create radical improvements in effectiveness or find new value through synergy.

Also important is an outside in view or using the customer lens. How might the customer experience your processes? In addition, supply chain or broader eco-system partners will have valuable insights into improving your end-to-end processes. Given that they are often on the receiving end of your inefficiencies and often see what you can't, makes their external view critical. It is worth exploring the art of the possible from their perspective.

Seeking execution effectiveness opportunities and synergies across the value chain, is a great opportunity to harness cross-functional teams mentioned earlier. Creating a team that can bring fresh thinking to effectiveness is a powerful tool. I have observed how seldom leaders simply ask the business about where they see gaps, frustrations, and prospects. Therein lies a great opportunity to rethink entire processes, remove wasteful steps, and unlock huge potential. I recall one leader sharing his effectiveness technique. He found the laziest person, showed them the value chain, and asked them to simplify it, which they often did, as they hated wasted effort.

Creating the freedom for teams to rethink the end-to-end value chain effectiveness often produces extraordinary results. I have observed how the removal of unnecessary steps can radically simplify processes and effectiveness, resulting in improved business outcomes. I have seen countless examples of processes or ways of working that were created over long periods of time, and because nobody challenged it, they become engrained, sometimes even complicated to cater for a once-off event, all of which ultimately drags down productivity.

I recall one profound example in the audit environment, where a particular accounting standard process took approximately fifteen hours to complete. When an intern asked for work, the audit partner gave him this process, and said go fix it. To his pleasant surprise, the intern, with a data scientist background, came back with an intelligence driven solution that took three minutes. Wow, and wow again. I always marvel at the speed of tyre changes in formula one motor racing. Half a century ago, the tyre change took at least a minute, now it is a shade under two seconds; in my view a classic example of end-to-end process effectiveness. It probably took you longer to let this point sink in than a full tyre change. Hopefully, this is food for thought.

Today there are also smart technologies which can analyse processes and related data to streamline efficiencies. Having said that, there is often a human element and a process element that requires people to change, and with that comes obvious reluctance. Creating a shared goal that everyone can get behind, explaining how everyone benefits and how it makes work more meaningful, often opens the opportunity to make simplification possible. As a word of caution, prior to making the changes, test the business impacts, risks created and unintended consequences. Once those are mitigated, then implement.

✗ Practical tools

A useful concept is to do a visual walkthrough of an end-to-end process, with a cross-functional and multi-disciplinary team. At each step ask, what are the recipient's needs, frustrations for all parties and therefore the opportunities. It is also key to ask what can be stopped. Another idea is to ask a customer or role play a competitor – what would you see, want, or do?

Other practical exercises could be to have a dialogue on how the following limit effectiveness:

- Selected individuals
- Difficult bosses
- Toxic team members
- Poor ways of working
- Bully culture
- Ineffective organisational structures
- Unnatural silos
- Old policies
- Outdated business processes
- Lack of systems
- External factors
- Unreasonable client demands
- Inappropriate governance.

I have often observed how the removal or changing of these factors can truly liberate an organisation and trigger a spurt of positive energy. Think about the typical obstacles mentioned above, and how some of those may be found in your organisation. How often have you heard, "If only management could see that this is a serious problem?"

Finding those bottlenecks and asking why they exist and how they can change is profound, and a huge source of value. As stated often, it requires an action to make it happen.

?

Question 11.3

DO YOU DRIVE EFFECTIVENESS THROUGH MEANINGFUL WORK?

⌐ *Key message*

Global statistics on disengaged employees are staggering. I believe that a key driver of this is that employees are in a rut because they are not motivated through meaningful work. Leaders have a critical role to play in creating an environment which is conducive to the design of meaningful work. If we are honest, then many of the jobs in organisations today are boring, routine and increasingly compartmentalised because of continuous process improvements, cost cutting, and system changes. Work has lost meaning for many, resulting in disengagement and lack of energy. From a sustainability point of view, leaders need to create meaningful work which will challenge, grow, and enhance human capabilities.

🗪 *Key action phrase*

Be intentional about creating an environment in which the effective design of meaningful work can take place.

⚠ *Warning signals*

* Employee engagement feedback is poor

* People are not energised or motivated by their work

* Employees are frustrated by mundane and routine tasks

* Process efficiency projects leave a bitter taste for many employees

♀ *Observations*

A few years ago, I came across a brilliant article, titled, "What is work?"[29] The title/question is rather profound. Shortly after reading this, I presented at a human resources conference, and started with this question: "As Human Capital executives you support meaningful work, but before we start, what is work?" There was a stunned silence, followed by a fascinating debate on the question.

Sadly, as we think about work and many jobs today, they are a consequence of numerous interventions over the years, often with good intent, but with harmful long-term outcomes. Think about what cost reduction, outsourcing, standardisation, shared services, transaction centres, process designs, and countless system implementations have done to jobs. Often the work and job have lost meaning and limited our human capabilities. Obviously, many other initiatives have sparked new work, jobs, innovation, and totally new careers.

Therefore, before we ramble on about meaningful work, or what work really is, it is probably more relevant to consider what *work* should be. In the same article,[30] "What is Work", it essentially describes redefining what work should be, by shifting employees' time, effort, and attention from executing routine tasks to identifying and addressing unforeseen problems and opportunities. I know this is the ideal state, but it does emphasise how critical it is to be deliberate about creating meaningful work for employees. In the long run if we do not unlock their passion and motivate them, everything will be in decline, including your organisation, your value proposition, and its sustainability. It goes without saying that work still needs to be aligned to the organisation's strategy and business outcomes.

Would you want routine boredom, or work that involves creativity, passion, solving, serving, innovating, and making a difference? No prizes for where most votes will go. It is therefore a leadership imperative to create an environment which is conducive to allowing the organisation and teams to re-design work that will enhance the employee experience and ensure organisational sustainability.

Meaningful work could include some of the following descriptors: be stimulating, unlock passion, harness innate human capabilities, exercise creativity, create solutions, make an impact, and maximise human potential. Expanding on human capabilities, it describes human attributes which are not reliant on context and can be demonstrated, maximised independently, and can be grown over time. Examples could include creativity, conceptual thinking or problem solving.

Perhaps one common example to many roles is the spreadsheet and manual reconciliations. The reality is that for most individuals, this is not meaningful work. If given the opportunity many would rather analyse for insights, visualise data, tell the story or collaborate with colleagues to add business value.

🛠 *Practical tools*

Some practical considerations for redesigning work for meaning:

- Define jobs to be done/outcomes to be met
- Define how it can be most simply completed
- Analyse what does not work and identify root causes
- What can be changed, amended, automated, or stopped?
- What can be changed to make the work more human orientated?
- How can human capabilities be harnessed?
- How can technology be used as an enabler?
- Redesign work, job, and roles to create meaning.

Question 11.4

DO YOU FOCUS ON THE RIGHT THINGS AND HOW WELL YOU ARE DOING THEM?

⚯ *Key message*

Leaders should create clarity on what really matters for the organisation and consequently where the focus should be. This may sound simplistic, but it is surprising how few leaders can clearly articulate what the activities are that really matter, versus those which are inconsequential. It also follows that leaders need to define what great looks like when the right activities are done well. Managing performance can then be focused on how well you are doing the right things. Having clarity on what really matters is critical to focus collective energy.

🗩 *Key action phrase*

Focus performance on what really matters and how well they are being executed.

⚠ *Warning signals*

- The organisation is not getting the results it expects
- Individuals or teams appear to be doing their own thing
- Performance results are inconsistent
- Teams often do seemingly random things

⚲ *Observations*

It often surprises me how often leaders do not seem to understand what makes their teams succeed or how they obtain good results. This often points to the fact that leaders are not clear on what the right things are that the organisation needs to focus on. They do not ask why they obtain the results they do or what really matters. If the leader is not clear on what really matters, then it is unlikely that the manager levels will know.

A leader's ability to know what the right things are, articulate it, and ask probing questions on how well the organisation is doing those things is often overlooked as a strategic tool. It demonstrates that the leader has deep insights on what drives the business, from a systemic point of view.

Prior to creating clarity on what the right things are, the leader needs to understand what outcomes are being driven and/or what problem is being solved. These aspects have been covered in previous questions. In this context, leaders should step back and truly decipher what the right things are that an organisation needs to do, like the discussion on golden threads earlier in the book. The value of a leader can be reflected in their ability to clearly articulate this to the business in such a way that the energy and efforts of teams and individuals is focused with razor like accuracy.

Describing this capability is difficult but think of times when a leader cuts through complex conversations and makes a radically simple statement, synthesises a difficult issue, or asks that deeply probing question that stops everyone in their tracks. These leaders know why they get the results they do. They know what matters most. Often when I facilitate a leadership team, they will see me write an acronym, WRM (what really matters) on the board. As a leader, you need to be clear on WRM.

To make the right things more impactful, it is essential to define what good looks like, or as Jim Collins would say, what great looks like. In the absence of what great looks like, mediocrity can creep in, and the status quo is retained. As mentioned earlier, at best you may get incremental results, rather than significant improvements. So, defining what great looks like is essential to improved outcomes.

Equally important is for a leader to identify the activities or processes that should be stopped, because they are wrong or do not add value. This is often harder to do than figuring out the right things. Having said that, often removing the wrong things, or the obstacles to effectiveness, can yield exponential improvements in overall performance. We have covered examples of this earlier in the book.

With clarity around the right things and what great looks like, it becomes easier to manage performance, and evaluate how well we are doing the right things. As always, the complexity is in the details and being very deliberate and consistently focusing on the effectiveness of the "how" and "what" you do, will deliver the desired results. What really matters?

⚒ *Practical tools*

Within the context of doing the right things, I love Peter Drucker's famous question: "Tell me what you are not doing?" My interpretation of this is what wrong things have you stopped doing, so that you can focus your energy on more of the right things. This awareness can be enlightening.

I challenge every leader, manager, or employee to conduct a self-assessment – does everything you do really matter? It is probable that each of us do things which are wasteful or irrelevant. What will you do about it, starting now? The table presented in the practical tools of question 9.4 is a useful tool to prompt this thinking.

Question 11.5

DO YOU RUN EFFECTIVE MEETINGS?

⛊ *Key message*

Meetings certainly come close to the top of the biggest frustrations for most executives. Almost without fail, every organisation will tell you they have way too many meetings. Effective leaders focus on limiting the drain of wasteful meetings. Effective meetings have clarity around focus, purpose, planning, participants, and logistics. Freeing up leaders from unnecessary meetings, allows them to focus on customers, employees, and other value-adding strategic opportunities.

💬 *Key action phrase*

Take deliberate action to make meetings efficient, effective, relevant, and impactful.

⚠ *Warning signals*

- There are way too many meetings in the organisation
- Everyone complains about meetings
- Often you wonder why you are in a meeting
- Most diaries are back to back meetings, all week
- Meetings are way too long

⚲ *Observations*

"I can't wait for tomorrow, so I can sit in a full day of meetings," is a quote I have never heard. In fact, if there is a consistent gripe from all leaders with whom I engage, then it is the drain on time and energy from way too many meetings. If every leader can free up half a day a week to work on the business, then that would reap significant results and outcomes. What often surprises me is how few leaders do something about it.

227

However, I have seen several organisations recently address this scourge.

Whilst I fully recognise the importance of meetings, engagement, and dialogue around critical matters, it is making the decision to drive effective meetings that is important for a leader. It is also important that for the benefit to materialise, it must be leader-led.

Below are some pointers for leaders regarding re-thinking meetings across the organisation.

- Focus
  - Determine the focus of the meeting, i.e., define a successful outcome
  - Meetings that focus on too many things are less effective and wasteful
  - Focus could include strategic, operational, brainstorming, engagement/information sharing, or lessons learned
- Planning
  - Effective meetings are always well planned
  - Unplanned meetings show it and waste a valuable resource, executive time
  - Planning considerations could include preparation, time, agenda, quality of pre-read or presentation, cadence
- Participants
  - Effective meetings only have the right participants attending
  - There is no greater tragedy than wasting executive time in mindless meetings. Do not invite people if they really do not need to be there
  - Select participants based on focus of the meeting, decision required, diversity of thinking, impact they bring or influence they have in executing
- Impact
  - Meetings should be impactful to the organisation, outcomes, and participants
  - Shorter impactful meetings are better than long drawn out affairs. Challenge the status quo (does it have to be four hours, or can it be three, does it have to be thirty minutes, or can it be twenty minutes?)

o Impactful meetings consider ways of working, managing participants, actionable minutes, and shift in organisational outcomes.

From an individual point of view, always question whether you really need to be at the meeting, or whether you were invited because it seemed right to the organiser or because some unwritten organisation policy said so. As a leader you have choices, so choose wisely how you spend your precious time.

Another interesting consideration is the physical venue – outside of our virtual world. The physical space can have a major impact on effective meetings. As a simple example, holding a brainstorming workshop in a stuffy windowless boardroom, is unlikely to yield the same results as an airy venue overlooking a garden or pond. Thinking about the physical space or virtual approach can have exponential impact on meeting outcomes.

A poor meeting culture is driven from the top. An effective meeting culture significantly contributes to value creation.

⚒ *Practical tools*

In thinking about your energy and effective meetings, a simple but powerful exercise could save ample time:

- Do a high level analysis of your diary for a month. How much time was effective versus wasted?

- Coordinate to be excused from those you do not need to be in

- Send a subordinate in your place

- Do not say yes to random meetings unless there is a clear focus, and you absolutely must be there. Saying no is often OK

- If you must attend a meeting, how do you leverage the time to get input or insights for your priorities?

This time saving can either be used for quality thinking time, or a cappuccino with a colleague. One sugar please.

PART 12

MANAGING RISK AND OPPORTUNITY

"One of the tests of leadership is the ability to recognize a problem before it becomes an emergency."

Arnold Glasow

Answer the following questions as accurately as possible, trusting the intuitive nature of your first response. The bonus question is intended as an outside-in view.

Part 12 – Question summary	Totally disagree	Disagree	Neutral	Agree	Fully Agree
12.1 Can everyone in the organisation articulate the top five controllable risks?					
12.2 Are you confident that the risk mitigation is actionable?					
12.3 Are you prepared for a crisis and able to create opportunities from it?					
12.4 Do you have a mindset of managing controllable risk to zero?					
12.5 Do your lessons translate into improved execution?					
Bonus question					
12.6 What would your competitors or ex-employees consider to be your biggest weakness?					

Once you have read this chapter, revisit your responses above and assess whether your responses remain the same.

What does this reveal to you? What three actions or goals are you going to set yourself regarding these insights?

?

Question 12.1

CAN EVERYONE IN THE ORGANISATION ARTICULATE THE TOP FIVE CONTROLLABLE RISKS?

⌐ *Key message*

This part of the book is deliberately titled managing risk, rather than risk management. This is a subtle, and yet important difference. Managing risk implies that you are proactive in doing something about it, while the latter implies that when it happens, you will then try and do something about it. Therefore, being clear about your greatest controllable risks and managing them effectively is a sustainability imperative. Managing risk is a proactive action, versus a reactive mitigation.

💬 *Key action phrase*

Ensure that the whole organisation can articulate the greatest controllable risks and align work efforts to manage those risks.

⚠ *Warning signals*

- When a key risk materialises, everyone is caught by surprise.
- Risk management is a tick box exercise to satisfy the Audit Committee.
- Senior leaders all have a different view on what the key risks might be.

♀ *Observations*

Mention risk management, and most executives will yawn with boredom, and will only pay attention when the risk manifests itself. Managing risk is a proactive approach that seeks to take controllable risks and manage them to zero, where viable. This can be done by operationalising risks into how you do business and is an effective way of reducing the impact of significant controllable risks on your business.

Leaders need to be clear about what the top five controllable risks are within the business. Using these five as a starting point, it is essential to create greater awareness of those risks, the impacts if they materialise and what collectively the business will do to mitigate them. Easy enough, but the real value then comes if you can operationalise the risk.

The first step is creating awareness about the most critical risks you can control. I believe it is essential to differentiate between what you can control and what you cannot. I will deal with non-controllable risks later. The greater the awareness of risks which can blow you out of the water and being prepared for them, the more resilient your business will become.

The next step to managing risk more effectively, is to operationalise the risk. Simply stated, this means instilling ways of working or processes which reduce the probability or impact of a risk materialising. This is often a lot easier than it being seen as a forced risk management practice.

I will use an illustrative example of operationalising risk, one which occurs in many organisations, that of developing a sales pipeline of projects. This example could apply to construction, consulting, engineering firms or simply delivering a capital project. It is well known in many industries that a key risk to delivering on projects is often not the execution itself but concluding the commercial contract. Once you have signed, and the project goes wrong, a poor contract is unlikely to protect you. To operationalise the risk, design ways of working and processes that ensure that your pipeline management and upfront commercial processes bring adequate rigour to reduce risk.

My experience, and that of many leaders I engage, is that one area where organisations get it wrong, is making risk management the responsibility of client or market-facing executives. The focus for this group of executives should be customers, market delivery or talent development. Whilst it is recognised that they carry ultimate responsibility for risk, the growing governance burden is shifting a disproportionate burden to these executives. It makes far more sense to invest in adequate support resources that provide the enablement that frees customer and market-facing leaders to drive revenue and growth, which are more value enhancing. The opportunity is often missed because of the excessive risk management focus. This may make it a lot easier for executives to embrace managing risk.

Finally, what is also important is the leadership tone, and the mindset which leadership brings to managing risk. Your attitude towards managing risk will set the tone for how your organisation responds.

✗ Practical tools

A very simple way of looking at risks, is thinking about a simple quadrant with probability on one axis and likelihood on another. Then plot controllable risks against the two axes and address those with the highest impact in the top right hand quadrant.

In addition, ensure that the organisation is clear on what appropriate risk responses could be. Risk response steps could include, accept, reduce, avoid, or transfer externally. This is addressed more fully in the next question.

Question 12.2

ARE YOU CONFIDENT THAT THE RISK MITIGATION IS ACTIONABLE?

⌘ *Key message*

There is a substantial difference between risk mitigation that works effectively and risk mitigation which is superficial. The difference lies in how organisations have approached the design of risk mitigation. Mitigation which is effective has been stress tested, is relevant to the circumstances and is intuitively actionable. The essence of effective risk mitigation is that when the risk manifests itself, everyone is clear on what actions they need to take to minimise the impact of the risk event.

💬 *Key action phrase*

Ensure that risk mitigations are stress tested, relevant and actionable.

⚠ *Warning signals*

• When a risk materialises, the organisation scrambles to find solutions

• Typically risk mitigation steps are found deficient when put to the test

• Risks often hit your business in a disruptive way

• Risk management is frowned upon, as it supposedly holds back business

⚲ *Observations*

I have no doubt that everyone can relate to a situation when a risk event took place, and the organisation went into a wild panic, trying to figure out what to do. What's even more interesting is the myriad of excuses that surface, to justify or support the fact that the risk mitigation failed.

Assuming that the risk cannot be transferred, then risk mitigation entails three steps: stress test the mitigation, ensure the response is relevant to the context and ensure that the risk is actionable.

An interesting way in which organisations stress test risk mitigation, is to conduct "war games" in which they simulate a risk event, and then stress test if the envisaged mitigation works or does not. By simulating an event, leaders can assess how robust the response is, and where gaps could be filled. It can also be useful to have someone act as an impartial referee to test if the mitigation would de-risk the situation or whether the action is superficial.

Next, it is also vital to see that the response is relevant to the circumstance or context, in other words, is it practical or realistic. In a crisis, there is no point in having a lengthy mitigation that takes days to activate, when the crisis requires immediate action within minutes.

Finally, the mitigation must be actionable, which implies clarity on what steps to take, who will take it, when, and how. Linked to this, the mitigation plan must be readily available, not stored somewhere on a server where it cannot be found. As a leader thinks through the actionability of the mitigation, they should consider whether the response is intuitive or overly complicated. The last thing you need when responding to a risk that materialises is for teams to be debating what was meant by the specific action or steps.

I do not think many organisations were prepared for what Covid did in 2020 to the office work environment. Forced national lock-downs left many people scrambling to respond. For many organisations this disrupted their business for months, whereas for others they were quickly able to adapt and move on. Therein lies a key point, when a risk materialises, is your organisation paralysed or are you able to respond and move on rapidly.

✗ *Practical tools*

In terms of risk mitigation, develop role play exercises, which get teams together with different roles and perspectives and simply run through key risk mitigations and ask if they are relevant, appropriate to the risk and actionable.

Based on the above-mentioned role play, enhance, or strengthen the mitigation.

Question 12.3

ARE YOU PREPARED FOR A CRISIS AND ABLE TO CREATE OPPORTUNITIES FROM IT?

⌐ *Key message*

Every organisation will face a crisis, and it is likely that crises will become more frequent as we enter an increasingly disruptive and complex world. It is imperative on leaders to develop a crisis response plan where everyone knows exactly what to do and how to respond. Whilst the immediate response is a critical moment that matters, what is far more fundamental, is how leaders guide the organisation beyond the immediate crisis and articulate the building blocks that allow the organisation to improve and even flourish post the crisis. Amid a crisis it is easy to neglect the opportunities that the crisis can create. Leaders that can change the lens on risk and ask profound questions could well create a new business opportunity, reduce cost, or improve margins.

💬 *Key action phrase*

Develop a crisis response plan that can minimise the impact of a negative event but also be deliberate in creating a mindset that seeks the opportunities created by the risks or crisis.

⚠ *Warning signals*

- The organisation struggles in times of crisis
- Leaders are slow to respond in a crisis
- Every crisis sets the business back substantially
- The brand and reputation take a knock after a crisis

- Nobody thinks about the opportunities that the crisis can create
- The organisation has never innovated because of a crisis

⚲ *Observations*

We have all observed how organisations respond during a crisis, either commendably or so poorly that we wonder whether the leadership were present at all. A crisis will often test how good your organisation is at managing risk. The last thing you want in a crisis is to panic while someone figures out where the plan was filed, or even if it exists at all.

Leaders need to ensure that they have a crisis response plan that can be instantly activated to minimise the impact of a negative event. This means not only a well-articulated response plan but also clarity on who does what, when and how in the event of a crisis. The ability to be proactive, take control of the situation and own the story is fundamental to a successful response plan. I want to stress the point on owning the narrative. Either own it or let others decide how the story is told. You have a choice after all. Owning the narrative is particularly pertinent in a visible and real-time social media world.

Leaders should spend time finding ways to improve their business and strengthen the organisational muscle, so that the impacts can be minimised in future. Great leaders will go beyond and think about how they can take advantage of the crisis and find new business or growth opportunities. A crisis or a risk presents an opportunity of flipping a crisis on its head and seeking business opportunities or how the organisation can capitalise on the risk to create competitive advantage.

This has the potential to either create opportunity for margin improvement or potentially even a new solution or business spin-off. Using the pandemic, think about how many virtual businesses either started or flourished as they adapted to the risk and started entirely new businesses. Some of the most obvious were virtual tools and on-line/delivery businesses, which served you when you were in lock-down, and chemicals companies that made sanitizers.

The essential message here is that for every risk or circumstance, there is a world of possibility when you change the lens. What world of opportunity exists for your organisation? Innovative organisations consider delegating opportunity management to a senior leader, despite the crisis. Their role is to step past the immediate crisis and find value opportunities.

Finally, many leaders and organisations are often caught off-guard in a crisis, allowing the crisis to dictate where decisions are made. I always say, never waste a good crisis. Great leaders anticipate a crisis, and when it does, take action that improves the organisation for the future. Leadership and organisational resilience are a muscle which can be worked on, and then leveraged when needed.

🛠 *Practical tools*

Working with leaders during a crisis, I often observe how they want to implement knee-jerk solutions. My practical advice is never making a long-term decision amidst a short-term crisis. These knee-jerk reactions often have a way of unravelling and in fact destroying value and credibility.

Conducting simulated discussions on risks and opportunities can often create insights that would not otherwise surface. De Bono's Six Thinking Hats is a useful tool for such simulated art of the possible discussions. Allocate team members to thinking through risk and seeing what opportunities can be created.

Whilst decisiveness in a crisis is essential, long-term impacts must be considered. Some questions to ask:

- What are the essential facts?
- What really matters?
- What decision is required?
- What is the risk of the decision and possible unintended consequences?
- What is the risk of not making a decision?
- What is the long-term impact?
- With hindsight, would the decision be intuitive and rational?

?

Question 12.4

DO YOU HAVE A MINDSET OF MANAGING CONTROLLABLE RISK TO ZERO?

⚊ *Key message*

In any organisation risk has a cost, and while some shrug their shoulders, leaders in successful organisations embrace risk as an opportunity to reduce costs and improve profitability. The fundamental difference is the mindset encouraged by leadership. Obviously, this does not apply to all risks, but should be considered for those risks which have a high probability and if it happens will have a high impact. In this case, it is worth focusing on this as a margin enhancing opportunity.

🗩 *Key action phrase*

Encourage a mindset that manages risks to zero, where viable to do so.

⚠ *Warning signals*

- You allow risks to manifest, and grudgingly accept the costs.
- Your organisation accepts that bad things cost you money.
- Your organisation only practices risk management.

♀ *Observations*

Many businesses budget for risk to happen, whether in their businesses or projects. Leaders in these businesses see it as a cost of doing business, and often determine that it is not worth their while to fight it. My view is that it comes down to mindset towards the risk. Using an example of a capital project, organisations often allow for risk or contingency of say five percent. Many organisations will simply ignore it and intimate that they knew it was coming and so take little action to avoid it. Let us pause on that for a moment. How often can you save five percent of the cost of a capital project? How difficult is it to target a five percent margin improvement? Taking that a step further, imagine the value of all projects if a five percent risk could be avoided?

Leaders therefore have an opportunity to view controllable risks with a new lens, that is a mindset that the risk allowable is a value opportunity. I have seen this in many project-type businesses, where being proactive on managing risk, has yielded substantial margin uplift. This thinking can even be applied to any other controllable risks. If a risk will cost you five percent, then it may well be worth spending one percent to reduce the risk and bank the difference. It could be the difference between a failed business or a sustainable business. My experience is that if a risk allowable in project related businesses and in capital projects is not managed effectively, then as the risks materialise, the negative value impact tends to increase significantly, and often the final cost is substantially greater than the initial contingency.

Therefore, being deliberate in creating a mindset that managing risk is a proactive management function rather than reactionary control task, can make all the difference. This mindset could also have other positive spin-offs.

⚒ Practical tools

The next time you have a project or similar event which has a risk or related contingency, allocate dedicated resources to managing the risk to zero. Do not be scared to spend a little to save a lot.

Question 12.5

DO YOUR LESSONS TRANSLATE INTO IMPROVED EXECUTION?

⊶ *Key message*

We all know that a lesson does not become a lesson learned until it changes behaviours, processes, and improves execution, on a sustainable basis. It is fascinating how organisations can repeat mistakes multiple times and remain hopeful that it will not happen again. Again, changing behaviours, actions, processes, and systems requires deliberate action from leaders. Conducting lessons learned reviews or post project or after event reviews is good practise. Truly learning from mistakes is a value driver.

🗩 *Key action phrase*

Drive lessons learned processes that lead to sustainable changed behaviours and actions.

⚠ *Warning signals*

- Your organisation repeatedly makes the same mistakes
- Lessons learned exercises are performed, but nothing is done about it
- Post project reviews focus mainly on who to blame
- Individuals disregard previous lessons because they know better
- Mistakes or errors have led to disastrous financial results

♀ *Observations*

Most organisations have some or other form of lessons learned process within their business. These processes also go by different names: lessons learned, project reviews, after event forums or documented findings. These processes are often triggered by a nasty event or are required by some Board committee.

Often the processes exist, but the gathered information goes into some file server or is added onto a lengthy list of previous lessons. I have done two large-scale lessons learned reviews for mega capital projects over recent years. In the first instance, the lessons learned was an extensive, but cumbersome excel spreadsheet of *circa* two thousand lessons. Sadly, it was just that, a spread sheet, which was filled in so the manager could tick the box. In the second case, the lessons were captured in a comprehensive document covering over a thousand pages. The common finding in both, was the issues or lessons kept repeating themselves, despite detailed information being available on previous lessons. In both these reviews, the biggest root cause emanated from a poor culture and ill-defined ways of working.

The next critical step is to create a meaningful lesson learned process. This is summarised in the practical tools below. This process is only useful if lessons learned consistently changes behaviours, processes, and improves execution, on a sustainable basis.

A primary root cause of lessons not being learned, is culture. Unless the culture and leadership behaviours truly onboard the teachable moments from previous lessons, then the same mistakes are likely to repeat themselves. A few key considerations for addressing culture could include:

- Ensuring that the lessons learned process is seen as a critical management function

- Prior to starting any new project or initiative, consideration is given to previous lessons

- Leaders are deliberate in changing processes or behaviours that caused previous mistakes

- Lessons learned reviews are seen as teachable moments

- True root causes are fundamentally dealt with

- Leaders who ignore lessons learned, face consequence management.

Finally, while collecting lessons is vital, the data should be turned into insights that can make a difference. Therefore, the lessons which really matter should be surfaced and changes must be made to behaviours and processes.

✄ *Practical tools*

Lessons learned should encapsulate the following elements:

- Define the issue – what was the impact

- Identify the root cause – what are the facts

- Conclude observations – summary of circumstances

- Define lesson – what is the teachable moment

- Rectification – what is the recommendation for rectifying the lesson

- Implementation – changed processes or systems for improved execution

Lesson learned – when behaviours and actions change.

EPILOGUE – PLAN A

"Success means using your knowledge and experience to satisfy yourself. Significance means using your knowledge and experience to change the lives of others."

Bob Buford

This book has been primarily focused on your productive life as a leader within an organisational context. I am hopeful that your time was impactful and that each of you were able to leave a meaningful legacy.

A final role a leader has in an organisation is knowing when to step down. We have all observed how leaders cling to power, whether as leaders in organisations or in political positions. True wisdom and impact can be demonstrated by stepping aside so that the next generation of leaders which you have nurtured, can take over. For many leaders, their leadership roles are often a huge source of energy and purpose and letting go is hard. Obviously, if you are privileged to be in a role where you are fulfilling a greater purpose, and you are still making a significant impact, then please continue. If not, then it is time to move to plan A, where you can make an even greater impact.

However, letting go of something which has been a large part of your life can be a huge disruption, and hard to do. I often hear of senior executives who after a hectic corporate life, go into retirement with no plans, other than maybe a few rounds of golf, and a bit of travel. Sadly, the number of cases of those individuals dying within a few short years is overwhelming. This is largely because they have not got a purpose after their corporate career.

Bob Buford in his book Finishing Well[31] talks extensively about living the second half of your life with purpose and leading a life of significance which is focused both on fulfilling your spiritual purpose, but also fundamentally about making a significant impact in the lives of others.

I therefore often ask senior leaders about their plan A. Initially I was surprised at how few had a plan or had even vaguely contemplated it. Now, when I get that blank stare, I know, and I can have a fruitful discussion about their next ten or twenty years. As someone once told me, we were not put on earth to sit and do nothing, although appropriate down-time is vital for body, mind, and soul.

I therefore urgently encourage you to be deliberate in creating your plan A. Some practical suggestions on doing this:

- Be deliberate in finding quiet time to truly reflect on what your purpose is
- Write it down
- Reflect on what your plan A career could be and how it can meet your purpose, be significant and positively impact others around you
- Write it down
- Reflect and test with trusted people in your life
- Refine what you have written down
- Pray over it, until you have absolute peace
- At the right time, put it into action.

This process can take weeks, months, or even years. That is fine. After all, you are defining what you will be doing for a decade, or two. I specifically also say, write it down. Simply thinking about it is in my experience nebulous. Only when you see the written word, does it really start to stir the heart, enabling you to find the essence of your purpose and plan A.

Finally, we are all here because we have a purpose. In the absence of purpose, life can become mundane, and the will to live a meaningful life will ebb away. I heard a beautiful story from an elderly gentleman sitting around a campfire at a bush lodge, who sadly never shared his name. He said, when you retire at say sixty years of age and you are working forty hours a week, draw a line from sixty to ninety, at which time you should be "working" for two hours a week. These two hours could be serving tea in church or anything for that matter, as long as you have a purpose and a reason to get out of bed and live. Having purpose he said, is one of the secrets to a beautiful and fulfilling life. How profound!

John Maxwell's quote strongly resonates with me, "Once you've tasted significance, success will never satisfy."

Live life with purpose, passionately, make a significant impact, and end with your life fruitfully lived.

BACKGROUND TO AUTHOR'S LEADERSHIP JOURNEY

As I reflect on writing about my own leadership journey, I realise that for some their season is early in life, for others it is in their later mature years, and for others somewhere in between. With over thirty-five years of experience, including *circa* fifteen years with Murray & Roberts and *circa* fifteen years with Deloitte, I realise they were all foundational to what is yet to come. I believe that my season to produce fruit is now in my second half.

My school years were underwhelming both academically and in extra-curricular activities. I played first team rugby, chess, and was also selected as a school prefect in my matric year, the latter being the first glimpse of my own leadership potential.

My early twenties were equally underwhelming at university, although I held a variety of leadership roles, whether on university house committees or captain of sports teams. I was frankly clueless on how to lead, but I always had an interest and a desire to do so.

My life changed forever in my mid-twenties when I broke my neck playing rugby and was almost paralysed. My mother's prayers, God's mercy, and my determination to walk again prevailed over my three year recovery. In my late twenties it began to dawn on me how fortunate I had been and a wake-up call that I needed to live life passionately.

My thirties were more a reflection of how not to lead. As I now look back, I realise that my management style was dismal, and that I was lucky to get the results I did.

In my mid-thirties, I was privileged to attend Wharton Business School in Philadelphia for a few weeks. The Executive Development Program I attended was a catalyst for many changes in my life and career. One of the program directors, Michael Useem, dealt with the topic of leadership and signed a book for me with the words, "With best wishes for those leadership moments of your own." This program led me to leave a CFO corporate role for the first time and venture into management consulting and private equity.

During the early 2000's I supported the creation of a new mining platform in Murray & Roberts, delisting a mining business, and restructuring the legacy businesses. This required many organisational changes, numerous critical people moments and a variety of process and systems changes. I was very blessed to work with Henry Laas, who was the Managing Director of the platform at the time, and now CEO of Murray & Roberts. I believe that he was the first leader to see my true potential and do something to unlock that potential. This involved working with an executive coach, Godfrey O'Flaherty, who started steering me onto a new people journey.

Being a director on the Gautrain Rapid Rail civils project was another step-change in developing insights into leadership, both from a people point of view, but also a fundamental crash course in organisational culture. Besides being an unbelievable project to work on, it proved to be a treasure trove of leadership insights. I will always fondly remember the project, and the mega project employee engagement initiatives I delivered with the HR team.

Post Gautrain, I spent a few more years in the construction industry. During this time, I worked under Luc Jacobs, who was open to exploring leadership, team effectiveness and the value of culture. Together we experimented and grew. Luc also introduced me to my second executive coach, Elana Godley. Her passion for developing others and finding their potential was life-changing, and it made a significant impact on who I was to become. Her most important message to me was, "Remember to be your authentic self."

I returned to management consulting in 2014 and became exposed to the Deloitte CFO Transition Labs early on. I really took to it and thoroughly enjoyed facilitating those leadership interventions. This proved to ignite the next spark in my own leadership journey. Over the next few years, I was privileged to run many C-suite leadership interventions and ended up facilitating leadership discussions across the C-Suite, Boards, and senior management teams. Deloitte also gave me the opportunity to change careers from finance to human capital and leadership services. During this time, I facilitated leadership sessions with dozens of blue chip organisations across Africa and in Europe and the United States, giving me rich insights to leadership around the world. It also allowed me to learn from the truly heart-warming stories of many great leaders.

I subsequently joined MAC Consulting to focus on building a unique leadership business.

In recent years, I have also prayed extensively about my greater purpose in life. God has clearly shown me in countless ways, that my purpose is to develop the leaders of the future. Whilst I was never destined to become the CEO of a large business myself, God has equipped me over many years to the point where I am able to fulfil my purpose of leadership development and focus on leadership and executive effectiveness. I am encouraged and motivated to know that for each leader I can influence in a positive developmental way, that many more people will be indirectly impacted. Living my God-given purpose works for me, and ensures I wake up each day ready to make a difference. I could never have imagined this leadership journey, but I would not trade it for anything.

May God steer you in your own impactful leadership journey.

ACKNOWLEDGEMENTS

I would like to take this opportunity to thank and show gratitude to those who helped make this book a reality.

My wife Esmé, and sons Calvin and Bradley, for their unwavering support of my writing.

Readers of my previous fiction novels, who gave me the encouragement to keep writing.

A special thank you to my beta readers: Fortune Gamanya, Trisha Naicker, Jolandi Yeates, Mike Seymour, Carel Anthonissen and Richard Longe. Each of you brought unique insights, constructive challenge, and honest feedback. Thank you for your time.

A huge thank you and shout-out to my editor, Genevieve de Carcenac for her commitment to another book, her guidance, shaping my writing style, the richness of her inputs and insightful amendments. As always, a huge thank you and appreciation for your time. You have a beautiful gift.

God for my talent.

NOTE FROM EDITOR

In this book, Dave van der Merwe has managed to consolidate his considerable leadership experience into a practical and reflective guide. The author has not only gained this rich experience first-hand, but also through innumerable hours of focused conversations with many different leaders – some good, and some less so, but all having left him with memorable learning moments. Dave has included many personal anecdotes, which not only add richness and relatability, but bring concepts he discusses to life.

Reading this book has challenged some of my personal thoughts on leadership. I've enjoyed forming my own learnings as Dave has shared his. In my roles as team leader and coach, Dave's thoughts on personal values and authenticity particularly resonated with me. He offers some practical advice on how authentic leaders can "show up" to those they interact with. Furthermore, this well-structured and practical guide provides the reader with plenty of reminders to contemplate how their responses to the content could influence their day-to-day behaviour, and what changes they should make as a result.

Dave's thought-provoking learnings and reflections have been distilled into a well-structured guide for leaders at all levels, irrespective of how far they might have already progressed along their own leadership journeys. Although focused largely on business leaders, this book is recommended to anyone wishing to enhance or reflect on how they frame what effective leadership means to them, and how to become such leaders themselves.

Genevieve de Carcenac

REFERENCES

Buford, B. (2004). *Finishing Well: The Adventure of Life Beyond Halftime*. California: Zondervan.

Buford, B. (2014). *Drucker & Me: How Peter Drucker and a Texas Entrepreneur Conspired to Change the World*. Franklin, US: Worthy Publishing.

Collins, J. (2001). *Good to great*. London: Random House Business Books.

Covey, S.R. (1989). *The 7 Habits of Highly Effective People: Powerful Lessons in Personal Change*. New York: Free Press.

Covey, S.R. (2003). *Principle Centered Leadership*. New York: Free Press.

Coyle, D. (2018). *The Culture Code: The Secrets of Highly Successful Groups*. London, UK: Penguin Random House.

Gibbs, G. (1988). *Learning by Doing: A Guide to Teaching and Learning Methods*. Oxford Polytechnic, Oxford: Further Educational Unit.

Hagel, J. & Wooll, M. (2019). What is Work. *Deloitte Review, 24*. Available from: https://www2.deloitte.com/content/dam/insights/us/articles/5113_DR24_What-is-work/DI_DR24_What-is-work.pdf

Kline, N. (1999). *Time to Think: Listening to Ignite the Human Mind*. London: Cassel Illustrated.

Lencioni, P. (2002). *The Five Dysfunctions of a Team: A Leadership Fable*. San Francisco: Jossey-Bass.

Maxwell, J. (n.d.). *John Maxwell Quotes: Inspirational Words of Wisdom*. Available from: www.wow4u.com/integrityquotes

Maxwell, J.C. (2010). *Everyone Communicates, Few Connect: What the Most Effective People Do Differently*. Nashville, Tennessee: Thomas Nelson.

Ready, D.A. (2019). *Why Great Leaders Focus on Mastering Relationships: Great leaders are distinguished by their ability to master personal relationships*. Available from: https://sloanreview.mit.edu/article/why-great-leaders-focus-on-mastering-relationships/

Schmidt, E., Rosenberg, J. & Eagle, A. (2019). *Trillion Dollar Coach: Leadership Handbook of Silicon Valley's Bill Campbell*. London: John Murray Publishers.

Schwartz, J. with Riss, S. (2021) *Work Disrupted: Opportunity, Resilience, and Growth in the Accelerated Future of Work*. Hoboken, New Jersey: John Wiley & Sons Inc.

Sinek, S. (2009). *Start with Why: How Great Leaders Inspire Everyone to Take Action*. New York: Penguin Books.

Slap, S. (2010). *Bury My Heart at Conference Room B: The Unbeatable Impact of Truly Committed Managers*. New York: Penguin Random House.

ThoughtLeaders, LLC. (2019). *Start Building Your Leadership Fitness Today*. Available from: www.thoughtleadersllc.com/2019/12/start-building-your-leadership-fitness-today/

Tolle, E. (1999). *The Power of Now: A Guide to Spiritual Enlightenment*. Vancouver, Canada: Namaste Publishing.

Warren, R. (2002). *The Purpose Driven Life: What on Earth Am I Here For*. California: Zondervan.

Zander, R.S., & Zander, B. (2002). *The Art of Possibility: Transforming Professional and Personal Life*. New York: Penguin Books, 2000

Zenger, J.H. & Folkman J.R. (2009). *The Extraordinary Leader: Turning Good Managers into Great Leaders*. New York: McGraw Hill.

ENDNOTES

1   Buford, B. (2014). *Drucker & Me: How Peter Drucker and a Texas Entrepreneur Conspired to Change the World.* Franklin, US: Worthy Publishing.

2   Tolle, E. (1999). *The Power of Now: A Guide to Spiritual Enlightenment.* Vancouver, Canada: Namaste Publishing.

3   Covey, S.R. (2003). *Principle Centered Leadership.* New York: Free Press.

4   Slap, S. (2010). *Bury My Heart at Conference Room B: The Unbeatable Impact of Truly Committed Managers.* New York: Penguin Random House.

5   Warren, R. (2002). *The Purpose Driven Life: What on Earth Am I Here For.* California: Zondervan.

6   Maxwell, J. (n.d.). *John Maxwell Quotes: Inspirational Words of Wisdom.* Available from: www.wow4u.com/integrityquotes

7   Maxwell, J.C. (2010). *Everyone Communicates, Few Connect: What the Most Effective People Do Differently.* Nashville, Tennessee: Thomas Nelson.

8   Ibid.

9   Covey, S.R. (1989). *The 7 Habits of Highly Effective People: Powerful Lessons in Personal Change.* New York: Free Press.

10   Kline, N. (1999). *Time to Think: Listening to Ignite the Human Mind.* London: Cassel Illustrated.

11   Schmidt, E., Rosenberg, J. & Eagle, A. (2019). *Trillion Dollar Coach: Leadership Handbook of Silicon Valley's Bill Campbell.* London: John Murray Publishers.

12   Gibbs, G. (1988). *Learning by Doing: A Guide to Teaching and Learning Methods.* Oxford Polytechnic, Oxford: Further Educational Unit.

13   Covey, S.R. (1989). *The 7 Habits of Highly Effective People: Powerful Lessons in Personal Change.* New York: Free Press.

14   Kline, 1999.

15   Covey, 1989.

16   ThoughtLeaders, LLC. (2019). *Start Building Your Leadership Fitness Today.* Available from: www.thoughtleadersllc.com/2019/12/start-building-your-leadership-fitness-today/

17   Coyle, D. (2018). *The Culture Code: The Secrets of Highly Successful Groups.* London, UK: Penguin Random House.

18   Maxwell, 2010.

19   Sinek, S. (2009). *Start with Why: How Great Leaders Inspire Everyone to Take Action.* New York: Penguin Books.

20   Lencioni, P. (2002). *The Five Dysfunctions of a Team: A Leadership Fable.* San Francisco: Jossey-Bass.

21 Schwartz, J. with Riss, S. (2021) *Work Disrupted: Opportunity, Resilience, and Growth in the Accelerated Future of Work*. Hoboken, New Jersey: John Wiley & Sons Inc.

22 Zenger, J.H. & Folkman J.R. (2009). *The Extraordinary Leader: Turning Good Managers into Great Leaders*. New York: McGraw Hill.

23 Schwartz with Riss, 2021.

24 Ready, D.A. (2019). *Why Great Leaders Focus on Mastering Relationships: Great leaders are distinguished by their ability to master personal relationships*. Available from: https://sloanreview.mit.edu/article/why-great-leaders-focus-on-mastering-relationships/

25 Zander, R.S., & Zander, B. (2002). *The Art of Possibility: Transforming Professional and Personal Life*. New York: Penguin Books, 2000

26 Maxwell, 2010.

27 Collins, J. (2001). *Good to great*. London: Random House Business Books.

28 Kline, 1999.

29 Hagel, J. & Wooll, M. (2019). What is Work. *Deloitte Review, 24*. Available from: https://www2.deloitte.com/content/dam/insights/us/articles/5113_DR24_What-is-work/DI_DR24_What-is-work.pdf

30 Ibid.

31 Buford, B. (2004). *Finishing Well: The Adventure of Life Beyond Halftime*. California: Zondervan.

INDEX

learning and seeking, 43, 54
life and work, 1, 10
living a balanced life, 1–2, 4

M

make the community a better place,
130, 141
making strategic choices, 152
managing controllable risk, 230, 240
meaningful work, 100, 212, 221–223

N

new ways of doing things, 43, 54

O

optimal decisions, 191, 197
organisational values, 67, 69
organisation's value proposition,
152, 161

P

people's full potential, 110, 112
people's passion and strengths, 110,
116
performance management, 106, 112,
116, 118, 191, 195, 205–207
powerful questions, 21, 33, 48, 105,
122, 191, 193–196
purpose and aspirations, 152, 154,
156–158
purpose-led, in life and work, 1, 10

Q

quality thinking time, 22, 36–38, 46,
48, 59, 194, 210, 229

R

reflecting on self, 1
resilient, 43, 58, 60–61, 76, 233

resource allocation principles, 82,
152, 164
risk and opportunity, 215
risk mitigation is actionable, 230, 235
robust decision-making processes,
191, 197

S

servant leadership, 130, 137–140
setting the tone, 67
shared purpose, 88, 90–94, 154, 156
solve real business challenges, 191,
209
sounding board, 28, 43, 63, 65
stakeholders, 60, 63, 91, 93, 128,
130, 132–134, 137–139, 152,
154–155, 169, 171, 173–175,
184–185
strategic choices, 64, 133, 152, 158–
160, 167–168, 171, 173–176
strategic intent and tactical
execution, 212
strategic narrative, 52, 152, 159, 168,
190
sustainable value creation, 171, 173,
184, 190

T

talent for future capabilities, 110, 123
talent potential, 110, 142, 185, 187
team effectiveness, 88, 96
teams' discretionary energy, 88
think tank, 43, 63, 65
top five controllable risks, 230, 233
top five value drivers, 171
top five value inhibitors, 171
top priorities, 43, 45

U

unfiltered information, 191, 201
unlock people's full potential, 110,
112

www.ingramcontent.com/pod-product-compliance
Lightning Source LLC
Chambersburg PA
CBHW060336200326
41519CB00011BA/1957